Remember, It's OK

Loss for Teens

ISBN: 978-1-990336-36-2

Editor: Allister Thompson

CHICKEN HOUSE PRESS
282906 Normanby/Bentinck Townline
Durham, Ontario, Canada, N0G 1R0
www.chickenhousepress.ca

The authors are gratified that you chose this book to be with you during your grief. Please consider leaving a review wherever you bought the book, or tell others about *Remember, It's OK: Loss for Teens*. We can all help and support each other in the grief journey.

Dedicated to Pat, who took his teenage life.

OTHER BOOKS IN THE REMEMBER, IT'S OK SERIES

Loss of a Partner

Loss of a Parent

Loss of a Child

Loss of a Sibling or Friend

Loss of a Pet

THE REMEMBER GUIDEBOOKS

(to be used with any Remember book)

Guidebook One - A New Paradigm for Grief

Guidebook Two - For the One in Grief

Guidebook Three - For the Support Person

Guidebook Four - 8 Session Program for Grief

—free to download from the authors' websites—

Table of Contents

9   Foreword

11   About This Book

12   Acknowledgements

15   Red Moments

63   Orange Moments

103   Yellow Moments

126   Blank Pages for Your Story

137   Green Moments

159   Turquoise Moments

185   Pale Blue Moments

214   Blank Pages for Your Story

225   About the Authors

226   Testimonials

Remember, It's OK

Loss for Teens

MARINA L. REED
MARIAN GRACE BOYD

CHICKEN HOUSE PRESS

FOREWORD

My Dear Reader and Fellow Warrior,

As I sit here typing out this foreword, I can't help but feel how this is a such a fitting cosmic array of events in which I get to commemorate my own journey as I see you off on yours.

What a beautiful opportunity to honour my own loss and struggle.

This book, *Remember It's OK: Loss for Teens*, reflects the journey of my life, and I believe it will also reflect your own journey and that you may find yourself represented within these pages. This leads me to one of my biggest realizations: we are all connected by loss. And we still struggle to be understood and find a voice for our pain. Marina and Marian know that. And they did something about it. You will find your voice in these pages. Huge gratitude to them for this work.

Growing up without my father was a daily struggle, and in many ways, it still is. I think of him often, and missing him never takes a time out. When I was a teenager, I really struggled with the pain that I was carrying around. This translated into skipping school and experimenting with drugs and alcohol as a means of escape from the pain. It was hard for me to connect with people because they just couldn't understand such an event that changed the entire direction of my life. My loss expressed itself over and over: walking through my neighbourhood and seeing dads pick their daughters up from school; dads playing with their kids at the park; seeing my friends' dads helping them move into their new apartment, or help them paint and renovate their new business space, etc. Almost every day, I found myself wondering who might I be if I had that kind of help and support in my life.

My friends, this is no easy journey, I won't lie to you. Losing someone you love, whether that is a parent, a relative, a grandparent, a sibling, or a dear friend, is truly a loss that is forever. The pain doesn't magically disappear. You will often feel completely alone and as though no one understands what you have to deal with and will continue to deal with. But what you have now that I did not is this wonderful book. The authors understand how grief circles around us. We move in and around the colours of healing as they show in their book. It can be a comfort to you for a long time.

This book can be your support, your best friend, your voice of reason and understanding when the world around you seems terribly out of touch, oblivious, chaotic, and simply unrelatable. This book will make you feel understood and that you are a part of a community that is so much bigger than you or I as individuals. I survived and went on to create a path into education where I now help and teach young people. It was no easy task. And now I watch as other young people struggle and suffer with loss. I am so glad I can hand them this book. I believe it will accelerate their healing and allow them to know they are not alone. Help them understand themselves, teach them to think with courage and empowerment, learn to be strong and brave, allow them to feel their pain in safety. It will also help parents know how to help their child and how educators can truly be there for their students. We all need to learn how to embrace grief, for ourselves, and for each other. Grief knows no timeline, and we need to learn to support each other for as long as it takes. *Remember, It's OK* teaches us how to do that.

We are warriors. We make a choice, every single day, to get up and fight through the tears, the loss, the isolation, and the pain. We choose to honour the gift that loved ones we have lost gave us; we choose to live. We are infinitely stronger when we come together, share our struggles, and help one another carry them. That is what you have in your hands in this book: a community, voices sharing their pain, and guidance to bring you home.

There is incredible power in connecting and sharing our stories so that we may feel understood by others who carry the same weight. This book is now your community of support. Please understand that my support for you knows no bounds, whether we ever meet or not.

I hear you, I see you, I know your pain, and I will always be rooting for you, as are Marina and Marian.

I wish you nothing but love and light on your journey, and never, ever, ever forget that you are not alone.

With great love,

Brittany E. Wiessler
Surviving Teen
Honours B.A. Drama in Education, Psychology
B. Ed. Drama/Social Sciences

REMEMBER, IT'S OK: LOSS FOR TEENS

This book is written for teens, and teens have helped and guided us the whole way. Inside these pages are moments you will identify with and suggestions that will help you on this very painful journey through grief. Your grief. Your voice. This book can be your safety net, your comfort, your help. No secrets here. We will support you; remember, it's OK. We'll show you how.

You're not alone. Let us help you begin. Let us help you find yourself. Let us help you heal.

For parents and educators who want to help, in these pages, teens will tell you what they want and need, feel, and experience. Remember, it's OK.

ABOUT THIS BOOK.

Remember, It's Ok is an experiential book. You will live this book, not just read it.

Remember, It's OK is a series of books dealing with specific types of losses.

Whether you have lost a parent, a friend, a grandparent, or anyone you loved, we can help you. You are not alone.

We also want to mention that grief does not know religion or race or gender identification. We invite everyone to heal.

Grief is not a linear process. The 'stages of grief' were initially designed by Kübler-Ross to support palliative patients. It was never designed for people who have experienced loss. Rather than moving from one stage to another, grief is a journey that cycles back and forth, in and out, as you find your way. Please use this book to support how you feel, regardless of how much time has passed between now and when you experienced your loss. Explore the different colour sections and use the Moments that work for you. Go from colour to colour as you see fit, what works for you each day. You may find that you read all of Red two or three times, and even come back to it when you are at the end of the book, and that's OK. It is your journey.

Colours have universal themes that have resonated throughout history. The colour choices were instinctual for us from the beginning:

RED: survival, urgency

ORANGE: beginning to find self, immediacy

YELLOW: coming back to self, growing awareness

GREEN: learning to balance self, learning

TURQUOISE: what path am I on now, increased awareness and curiosity

PALE BLUE: clarity of new path, beginning to move forward, increased openness

We have left blank pages after the Yellow and Pale Blue Moments for you to insert your own personal story, drawings, reminders, photos, struggles, achievements, joys, and sorrows. We offer suggestions throughout the book on how to use these blank pages. There is a page dedicated to the Remember series at *marinalreed.com*, where we post resources to support you and comfort you on your grief journey.

We invite you to find healing in these pages.

There is a website dedicated to the Remember series. Please visit www.rememberitsok.com ot find where we post resources to support you and comfort you on your grief journey.

ACKNOWLEDGEMENTS

First, we would like to thank all the teens who spoke with us and helped us create this book that will speak to young people and those who need to care for them, as they are asking to be cared for. Your courage and honesty will inspire others. Thank you for trusting us with your story and your pain and your desire to heal. Thank you to Kaitlyn Wierenga, Kayleigh Robertson-Hart, Elly Furtney, Georgia Sideris, Brittany Wiessler, Edward Leslie, and Tyler Tucker for consulting with us on this project. We'd also like to thank Alla Valjero, a natural health practitioner, who kept us strong and healthy as we navigated these waters. To Allister Thompson for editing our manuscript in the masterful way that he does and to Alanna at Chicken House Press for helping us share the Remember series with the world. So much gratitude. And to our families, for your constant love, support, and encouragement. We could never have done this without all of you.

NOTE TO PARENTS

Ageism has no place in grief. Your child's pain is very real. Their whole being has been compromised. What they need is space, hugs, and consideration. Truly listen to them without question. Trust them. To understand how they are feeling, and thinking (and how difficult it is for them to concentrate and focus), please read this book, and consider the advice and tone of the companion. Give them their voice, not yours. Your child needs you now, more than you know.

NOTE TO EDUCATORS

Ageism has no place in grief. To tell a young person who is grieving that getting back to routine and assignments will help is fundamentally incorrect. A student in grief is not processing information correctly. They are not trying to "get out" of anything; they are in pain and need space and understanding. Often they are suffering from PTSD and need great support. In order for a teacher to know how to support a student, it is recommended they read this book. Attempt to take on the role of "companion" as we show in these pages. Education is far more than exams and assignments. Your students need you when they are in grief. We'll help you see how to do that. Remember, it's OK.

Red
Moments

I'm in grade 11. My dad died a year ago in a freak accident at work. I still can't believe it. I still wake up thinking it was all just a bad dream. And I guess it is, really, I mean he's dead, so it is a bad dream. Every day is a bad dream. It feel like he's everywhere but nowhere at the same time. I never say it out loud, but I hate it when my friends talk about their dads. Especially yesterday, when one was talking about how cool it was learning how to drive with his dad. Yah. Driving. Like, who's gonna teach me how to do that? Not my mom, that's for sure. I don't recognize my mom since my dad died. She's just not around, even when she's standing right there. My little sister isn't going to teach me. I miss my dad, but I'm also really angry at him too for leaving when he still had so much to teach me. I hate him. I really do. I hate him.

Yes, he still had so much he wanted to teach you. He would never have left you alone like this if he had a choice, that's for sure. It really, really sucks. And it makes sense that you hate him, hate this, right now. Your whole family is suffering. Death is hard, really hard. And you loved your dad, and that makes it so much harder.

I do love him. I do. I don't hate him, I just hate that he's gone.

I know.

I'm in grade 11. My dad died a few months ago. It's like I see danger every-where now. Just everywhere. And I feel scared all the time. Wonder what people are thinking or saying about me. When I tried to tell my brother, he just called me a name. My mom is a mess, so I can't tell her. But it's like the voices in my head are getting louder than real voices in the room beside me. Am I going crazy?

No, you aren't going crazy. Your dad's death was a huge loss for you, and it shook your world. Suddenly, nothing feels safe any more, like something big could hit you again. Yes, you will see danger every-where for a while. It makes sense. And it makes sense that you become hyperaware, on alert all the time. Those voices in your head are your voices, and it sounds like you are trying to find a way to talk about what is going on for you. That is exactly what you need to be able to do right now. Often, though, it's not our family who can handle our thoughts and grief, because they are grieving too. Do you have someone that you think would be able to listen?

I can't think of anyone, not right now.

Maybe at your school. Sometimes you can put in a note that says you want to speak with the school counsellor. Often, we just need to be able to say things out loud to someone. Not have them fix anything, just listen. How about that. Think you could give that a try?

Will it quiet these voices in my head?

It will help. It will be a good start.

I can't remember a day when Freckles wasn't there. I'm in grade 10 now. He was this cute little Springer Spaniel, and he was named freckles, well, because he had the cutest little freckles over his nose and under his eyes. Freckles. He'd sleep on my bed, and when I'd had a bad day, he'd come over and lick my tears away and lie really close to me. I'd secretly feed him little treats under the table, and we'd have this little smile between us. He'd help me with my homework and be waiting by the door when I came home from school. Then I came home one day, a couple of weeks ago, and Freckles wasn't there. Everyone was pretty quiet in the house. Mom said he'd been hit by a car and killed instantly. I wondered why no one had called to tell me or sent me a text. I didn't even get to say goodbye. And now, weeks later, everyone says it's silly for me to still be so depressed, but I am. I really am. And now I can't even say it out loud. Freckles was my best friend. I could tell him things I wouldn't dare tell anyone else. Now what do I do? I sometimes still talk to him. My parents are looking to get another dog, but that even makes me more sad and even angry. We can't replace Freckles. And I don't want another dog. But no one listens to me. No one except Freckles.

He was your best friend. So sad. I'm so sorry.

I wouldn't want another dog so quickly either. No dog will replace Freckles. We have the capacity for lots of love; we are able to love more than one animal or one person. Just keep that in mind, if another dog does come to live in your home.

In the meantime, why don't you have a little service for Freckles? You can bury his collar or something special to him. Light a candle and say something special for him. That way, you are saying he was important, and you are taking time to honour his life. Why don't you try that? It would be good for everyone who loved him. Can you suggest that?

Yah, I sure can. That's a great idea.

Blank Page Suggestion:
Write a goodbye letter to a pet you have lost. Tell them how much
you love them. Read it again when you are feeling sad.

My mom died six months ago. I'm in grade 10. It's hell. What can I say, pure hell. I'm a zombie at school, and everywhere in between. And when I get home, my dad's the zombie. My mom was such a great cook, she loved food, and we all loved to eat what she made. I loved loading the dishwasher with her, and it was often after she'd been cooking on the weekend. Now, it's take-out pretty much every night, on paper plates with plastic forks. I don't know if the dishwasher has even been turned on since she died. It's all gross. Someone told my dad to hire a cleaning lady; she does laundry too. Thank god for that. But Dad? He's gone. Like he's just gone. So there's no one to talk to, help with homework, help with anything . He took a leave from his work, and all he does is sit in Mom's chair in the living room. Just sits there. I don't know what to do.

Yes, it is a hard place. I remember when my husband died, all I wanted to do was sit in a chair. So I get that. That is pretty hard for you, though.

You are both suffering, differently, but you are both suffering. You may not have your dad to help you for a while. Is there someone else you can lean on, like an aunt or a grandma or a friend?

I guess I could ask my aunt for help.

Ask her. People will be there for you. They often don't know how, but if you ask, I'm pretty sure they will help as much as they can. Give it a try. And for yourself, can you maybe talk to a counsellor at school?

I guess I could do that. How would that help?

It will at least help you to talk out how you are feeling, sometimes just doing that helps.

OK, I'll try that. If I can stop crying.

You don't have to stop crying, not yet. Remember, it's OK. Maybe curl up on your mom's bed. What do you think about that?

Yah, I'd like to do that.

You do that, just for you.

I'm in grade 11, my first week. My best friend was taking one more week at her cottage. I just got the news last night. She flipped her Sea-Doo and died instantly. I still can't believe it. All the things we had planned for this year, for university, after. I think I threw up for three days straight. Then I just decided to go back to school. It was like an escape, really, where I just pretended. I don't think anyone else knows about the accident. No one says anything. And I'm sure not going to. Plus if I tell anyone, it won't be my escape from my pain; telling anyone will break that, and I like this pretend world.

Oh, I am so sorry to know that your friend had this accident and died. It sounds like she was very close to you. Thank you for telling me about it. I know it's hard even to know what to say, or who to talk to, or, as you said, if you even want to talk. Having a place of escape can feel important for a while.

I remember when a sudden loss happened to me, I wanted to cocoon myself away. Have my feelings just to myself and not have to share them with anyone else. I remember wondering who I would even talk to. I didn't want advice or someone else's story. I just wanted mine. I felt a good kind of selfish with my feelings. After a while, I began to poke my head out of my cocoon. I was ready to talk about my loss, but I sure had to look carefully to find someone that would just listen.

Right now, your cocoon is important and protecting you. Right now, that's exactly what you need. And that is OK.

Red Moment

I survived the car crash that happened a couple of months ago. I'm in first semester of grade 11. But three of my friends didn't. I don't think I'll ever be able to get their screams out of my head, and then seeing them just lying there, no movement, no life. And blood, so much blood, and metal squashed like tin foil. I've had nightmares about the crash over and over. We should never have gotten into that car. We'd all had too much to drink and smoke. I feel like it's my fault, that I didn't say anything, stop it all. I could have. But I didn't. Now they're gone. Like gone. No prom, no career, no life. Just gone. I was sent to see a therapist. The therapist talked a lot, prescribed me sedatives so I could sleep. They didn't help. In school and at home it feels like everyone is staring at me. Maybe they all blame me too. Maybe I should just end it too. I can't stand it any more.

As you speak, I can hear your love and your care for them. Oh, if you could get a do-over and change the story so that they were still here. The trauma of the accident just keeps circling around you. I was struck by what you said, "I was sent to see a therapist. They talked a lot..." Have you been able to talk? Talk to anyone about what happened and what you are going through now?

Right...me talk. No one listens to what I have to say. I'm dismissed. I'm JUST a teenager. My feelings don't seem to count.

Your feelings do count. For sure they do. It's not your fault. Even if you had spoken up, you don't know what the outcome could have been. It's hard to be left with the "what-if." It sure is. Here's something that will help. It really helped me at a desperate time in my life. Each time you begin to feel sad or desperate, stand very still and enter your five senses: at that exact moment what do you **feel** touching your skin, what do you **hear**, what do you **smell**, what do you **taste**, what do you **see**. Be very observant with yourself. It will help you be in your moment. It really will help. And breathe the whole time. You may have to do it a lot, and that's OK. Do it as long as you need to and as often. I remember doing it thirty or forty times a day until I started feeling better. Can you try that?

Yes, I will try that. That feels good, something I can hold on to.

Yes, hold on to it as long as you need to.

Blank Page Suggestion:
Write down things that you are experiencing with your five senses right now.

I'm in grade 11. I feel a mess of emotions right now; anger, resentment, guilt. They just keep playing around and around in my head. My mom had been in the hospital for a while, and we knew the end was coming. The waiting sucked. Just waiting for that last moment, to be there with her, I even worried about going to the bathroom. It had been days in a row, and my dad and aunt and sister decided to go and get something to eat at a restaurant next door to the hospital. It had been days since we'd had a good meal. The nurse said she had just given Mom a sedative, and she would probably just sleep while we were out. She insisted we go, take a break, said it would be good for us. So, we went. It was nice to get out of the hospital, although I felt a little guilty doing it. We got a drink, placed our order, and were just about to take a deep breath when our phone rang. It was the nurse, saying we should get back. We raced back to the hospital and to her room, but when we got there, she was already gone. All that waiting for nothing. I hated that nurse for sending us away. I was so angry at Mom for dying without us there. I couldn't even cry, I was so mad. I feel so guilty for leaving to have a meal when Mom couldn't come with us. Leaving her to die alone. I feel so awful.

Awful. Yes, I'm so sorry. How awful for you. I know you really wanted to be there with her. You know, sometimes a person who knows they are dying wants to protect those they love, even at that point. Sometimes they will wait until everyone is out of the room before they die, out of love. Did you know that?

No, no, I didn't. But I can see Mom doing something like that. Is there a chance the nurse was helping her by sending us away?

You never know, there are mysteries that no one can really answer at times like that. Did you have a chance to talk with your mom before she died?

Oh yes, we each took time alone with her and said what we needed to say. And then she wrote us each a letter. I guess she gave them to the nurse for when she died. The nurse gave them to us today. I'll keep that letter forever and forever.

Yes, I'm sure you will. It will always be a comfort to you. Is it in her handwriting?

Yes.

How very special.

I'm in grade 9. My brother just died of an overdose; he was two years older than me. I usually have my mom to talk to about stuff, but she is a mess. I've never seen her cry so much, and my dad, well, he's just gone silent. I wanted to tell my mom how I was feeling, but she never asked me, so I didn't say anything. I wanted to tell her and Dad that this isn't just their loss; I'm suffering too. But I seem to have become invisible. And there are so many regrets, and now we can't fix anything. His chapter is over. Death just seems so vivid all of a sudden. Like, no second chance. My brother wasn't bad, just because he died of an overdose. People don't know what they're saying. Makes me want to cut off my ears. I don't know how to deal with all these feelings. I don't know. I don't know what to do next.

Such a hard place to be and such a terrible loss. I'm so sorry. Of course he wasn't a bad person. People can say such thoughtless things. You want to be so real with all this, and you feel so alone. Death does make things vivid, so very true. And a lot of people can be really scared by that. But how do we look after you? What is it you need?

I need to be close to my brother somehow.

Is there a piece of clothing you can wear that was his? That can help.

That would be nice. I like that idea. I'll get one of his sweatshirts. That's a good idea.

And what about TV shows, what was his favourite?

Oh, he had a lot, but we liked to watch How I Met Your Mother *together. We laughed.*

I'm glad you can remember laughing with your brother. You know, often we can't fix things, we just can't, but we can hold those special memories close. Watching a TV show wrapped in your brother's sweatshirt will bring you some comfort, and right now, that is a lot. This is a time to really care for yourself, in any way you can.

OK, I wouldn't have thought of that. Thanks, thanks for caring about me.

It's second semester now. I'm in grade 11. My mom died six months ago. I feel all over the place and blurred. I need space, like, there is just so much homework, and that's all that seems to matter. No one even cares that my mother has died. Some teachers gave me extensions on my assignments, but how does that help? I can't do them, I can't do any of them. And more importantly, I don't want to. You know, I just want to sit, just sit, I just want to sit.

What an awful moment for you, the loss of your mom. It's so hard to find a way forward when you have experienced such a traumatic loss. How to just sit in a world that is spinning all the time. It's like there is no space. It's hard to know how to do that.

Here's an idea for you to consider. Think of your favourite place to be, and when you are there, you see a smile in your mind. For instance, my place is sitting beside a calm lake and hearing loons call to each other. And when my world starts spinning, I take myself to the edge of that lake and put that image into my mind, whether I'm in a bus station or a cafeteria, and I can have a moment where the world stops spinning.

Can you try that?

That's awesome. Thanks so much. Will do.

Blank Page Suggestion:
Write or draw the place that makes you smile. You can find lots of examples of nature scenes on Instagram to get ideas.

I'm in grade 12. I've been accepted to the university I wanted. Thing is, I don't care anymore. Everything changed when my parents died in an accident a few months ago. I wanted to work on environmental impacts. Make a difference. I always was involved in groups that supported the environment. My mom was really big on all that stuff. She got me interested and always pushed me to follow my passion. But I don't have passion anymore. Sort of like she took it with her when she died. And Dad was such a great sounding board. Now, it's all just quiet. My brother is finishing university. He's more quiet than ever before. Almost like he's gone too. I live with my mom's sister now. She's not like my mom at all. Residence in three months...if I go. I don't know what to do, what to feel, how I continue. I don't know. I don't know.

This is a life-changing loss for you. The things that you planned to do may not work for you now. Your main focus right now is to give yourself time to find healing in your pain. Truly, this will feel like a full-time job. You may want to consider getting an extension to your admission, give yourself time to find yourself, and your passion will follow.

I didn't think of that. That may be a good idea. I'll look into an extension. Thank you.

I'm in grade 11. My mom died a few months ago. Everything feels so weird now, kinda out of place, nothing fits. Sometimes when she'd had a long day, and I'd had a long day, and Dad was gone and my sister was in bed, we would sit together and watch a movie, eat a bowl of popcorn. So, one night when Dad was at work and my sister was in bed, I sat down and put Lion King *on, thinking it would be a comfort. I was not expecting what happened. Even though it is Simba's father and not mother that dies, I guess it was a parent, and I just couldn't stop crying. And I couldn't find the remote to shut off the TV. It was awful. I was almost hysterical. I'm scared to watch any movie now, so many have deaths of parents in them. I'm not sure what to do. My friends watch movies, my sister watches movies, I can't keep leaving the room all the time. I miss Mom. I miss her so much.*

Yes, I bet you do miss her. Your time watching a movie together sounds really special. It sounds to me like you have experienced a trigger. Do you know what a trigger is?

Not really.

It is when something happens to us right now, but it takes us back, as if we were back inside a memory, living it all over again. Triggers can be joyful or traumatic. You can read more about triggers on the Internet if you want to know more. This trigger for you, while watching the death of a parent in a movie, was overload, just overwhelming, and it's OK to step away. This is all so fresh for you. Give yourself some time, it's OK to do that. Not watching movies for a while will take pressure off you, especially if you feel nervous about what might be on the screen. You can only deal with where you are right now, and right now, watching movies is hard for you. Remember, it's OK.

Blank Page Suggestion:
Think of some things, or events, or smells that may trigger you in
a sad way, or in a happy way. Make a list. It will help you be more
prepared when they happen.

My dad died. I'm in grade 10. It's first semester. I can't do the work. And that's all anyone seems to care about. Assignments, exams. God, my dad just died. Doesn't anyone give a shit? Doesn't anyone know how I feel? Sometimes all I want to do is stand in the middle of the hall, while everyone is walking around in their perfect little bubbles, and scream at the top of my lungs.

Screaming at the top of your lungs is a good idea. I hope you can find a forest close by and let the trees absorb your pain. You will find safety there, and the freedom to scream as long as you need to.

Losing your dad, how heartbreaking. How horrible that no one seems to care that he died. And then to have to keep handing in assignments, how difficult. I'm so very sorry.

I had to go back to work after losing someone close to me, and I couldn't concentrate for more than a minute at a time. Here's something that helped me. I did my work in small chunks, little bits here and there, and then took breaks. Just work for as long as you can, and then step away, even if it's just in your mind. Would you feel comfortable asking teachers to allow you to leave the classroom when you need a break?

Not really. They seem consumed by rules, and if they don't listen it will just make things worse.

Right, I hear that. OK, so we have to figure out a different way. What is your biggest issue right now?

I guess my biggest problem is that I just can't seem to focus or concentrate. My mind just goes blank, and I hear this white kinda noise in my head.

Yes, I remember that feeling. Something that worked for me in those moments was a technique called tapping, and you can do it anywhere. It can help to rebalance you, even just for a moment, and then you can work. You can find videos about tapping on the Internet. It's really easy, and no one will even know what you're doing.

Grief is hard, and lonely. You are just beginning this journey. I'll help you.

OK, thanks. It's so good just to be heard and understood.

It would be great if schools and workplaces would accept how we feel when we experience trauma. That nothing else matters. Fewer assignments, more space, less fear. Hopefully that will come.

Meanwhile, we'll figure it out together. Give the tapping a try, remember to breathe, drink lots of water, and eat things you like. And chunk your work. How does that sound?

It actually sounds pretty good. I'm taking a breath now.

Good for you. You can do it.

I am in grade 10. My Grandpa, I called him Papa, wasn't very old. My mom had me when she was pretty young. Papa was really special, almost like a second dad. He had to go into the hospital to have this little procedure done, and was supposed to be home that afternoon. But we got a call from the hospital, and when we got to his room, he was already gone. He died. It's crazy, just crazy. Everyone was just standing there crying, my mom's sisters, my brother, me and mom. My mom was holding his hand, she went to kiss him, and we were all just watching Mom, and it felt like an invasion of his privacy; it was just all so weird. I didn't really know what to do, everyone was just standing there, my legs were like jelly, I felt out of my body. I was told I could say goodbye, but I didn't really want to. But I didn't want to cause a scene, so I picked up Papa's hand. It was cold but warm from where my mom's hand just was. I was starting to numb out. I can still feel that feeling of Papa's hand, but it wasn't his hand at all. I don't know if I'll ever get it out of my head. I kissed him goodbye, just quickly on his cheek. I was starting to feel really queasy, but I didn't want to throw up. And then we were walking out. Like walking out, just leaving him there, all by himself. Papa. We abandoned him. It's awful. I feel awful. I didn't even know who was moving my legs down the hall.

Not wanting to cause a scene, what a tough place to find yourself. Yes, I would feel nauseous too, kissing a corpse. Yes, tough stuff. I wouldn't want that to be the last memory you have of your Papa. How can we fix that?

I don't know, how?

Can you remember the last interaction you had with him before he went into the hospital?

Oh yah, it was at breakfast. And we were making little sentences with the cereal letters floating in the milk. It was hilarious, because he always made these inappropriate words, and when mom came into the room, we'd cover them with milk and snicker, almost blowing milk out our noses.

That's fantastic. Try to think of that anytime you think of him, instead of the hospital.

I'm laughing now. That's great. I sure will. Thanks. Great idea.

Blank Page Suggestion:
Write about a time you remember with the person who has died that was happy and fun.

I was in grade 10. My nana was living with us, had been for the past year. I loved Nana, even though she could be a bit of a pain sometimes. We were finishing up dinner, and Mom had gone to have a nap. I asked Nana if she wanted more tea, she said yes, and I moved to get the teapot. As I turned around, I saw her head slump forward onto the table. She became like a rag doll. I got this lump in my chest and was suddenly freezing cold. I started screaming for Mom. I couldn't move. Mom came in and started yelling at me to call 911. But I still couldn't move. Then everything became a blur, and I don't remember much. Except being cold and standing very still.

Oh, what a shocking moment that was for you! The shock totally froze you. That's what shock does. How is your Nana?

She's in the ICU. I don't know if she's going to be okay. It's pretty scary. And now, we're just at the hospital all the time.

And how are you doing?

I still feel cold. But I'm here at the hospital, trying my best. I don't know.

Is there any way you could get something warm to drink and a blanket? Maybe ask one of the nurses. Try to care for yourself.

Okay, I'll ask one of the nurses. Thanks for caring.

Red Moment

A universe that wasn't going to stop
It stole away friends,
family
No goodbyes
It lived on
my
grief
tears,
harm,
with no arms to reach out
to Faith
was lost
I needed hope
And I held on for so long
But one must break
One must fall
I need to breathe

Your words touch me. It's a hard place. You do need to breathe. Long, slow breaths. And while you are breathing, I will be your hope-holder.

Thank you, thank you so much.

Blank Page Suggestion:
Make a list of some people who can hold hope for you, until you can do that for yourself. And maybe draw or paste in a photo of an object that looks like it could hold hope. Write the word "hope" on a piece of paper and put it inside.

My dad was sick the whole time I was in high school. He finally died three days before I started grade 12. That's where I am now, at the beginning of grade 12, all a bit of a blur. I don't think anyone knew my dad was so sick, and I don't think anyone knows he has died. Frankly, I don't really know how to tell anyone. And I'm not sure if it would even help. Like I feel I'm telling this sob story, and I can't think of a logical reason to tell anyone, even if I did know how. So I just grit my teeth, say nothing, and carry on. I'm guessing the teachers got a memo or something. I don't know. I'm just doing the best I can, whatever that is.

Doing the best you can, good for you. It's all we can ever do. Consider this, though: there is a logical reason to tell your story and not just grit your teeth. And there is a way to do that. Firstly, it can be a release for pain we've stuffed down. It also makes us find other people who have a similar story, and they need someone to talk with as well. We don't achieve any of this if we don't talk to others. Remember, there are still cultures that wear black when someone dies. They do this so that they can talk with others openly and honestly about how they are feeling. I'm not saying you now have to wear black, but I am showing you that talking about our grief has always been important and still is. How do you do that? You speak from a true place of your pain, not a lot, just a few choice words, but that's how you begin. Who do you talk to? Someone you do know and do trust.

Blank Page Suggestion:
Be the one you trust right now. Use this page to speak your truth, say what you need to say, tell your story.

I'm trying to paint
My liver black with
Rum
Murals on these pages
With my words to fill
Anything that can't be said
Will be found at the bottom
Of the bottle
Carving meaning from
This half sung verse I
Yell into the lonely pages
Where my heart can be seen
Bleeding from these shattered, transparent
Dreams
Or maybe I can find a way
To fill the abyss that is fond
Of leaving gaping chasms
In my heart
Without filling this glass
And without
Filling inkwells with tears
Only to spill them
on this
Page.

Standing on the edge of an abyss is terrifying.

I don't know how to move.

Does finding the bottom of the bottle help you move?

No, not really.

Maybe you don't need to fill the abyss.

What then?

How about turning around, 180 degrees. What do you see when you do that?

Open space.

What's in that open space?

Water, lots of water. And sky, lots of sky.

So many possibilities.

OK, I didn't think of that, but yah, possibilities. Like what?

Well, the abyss will always be there if you turn around, and the possibilities will be there too. It becomes a choice. You can sail on the water, you can canoe, you can swim, and you can feel the blue sky and watch birds soar.

I like that. Right now, I think I'll sit and watch the birds.

That's a nice choice.

Blank Page Suggestion:
Make a list of your possibilities.

My friend killed herself the other day. Her mother was in and out of rehab. She's an alcoholic. I remember hearing her mother say she wished she had never been born, that she wrecked her life. I think I was all she had. I knew things were bad, but not that bad. I feel like it was all my fault. And now I am left with no one. Maybe she had the right idea. I mean, what is the point? I feel so alone here, no voice, no friend. I don't belong anywhere. I don't belong anywhere.

You *do* belong. Of course you do. It wasn't your fault. It really wasn't. You are in a hard place, for sure. It doesn't have to be like this forever. You can make choices for yourself now. You haven't lost everything. You still have yourself and adventures ahead of you. What do you want to do after high school? Any idea?

I don't know. My marks are pretty shitty. I don't know what I can do. And I don't see any point.

What do you like to do?

Well, I like animals and cars and bikes.

So there are programs you can do after high school where you can apprentice to work on cars, or bikes, or even with animals. You do have lots of choices. Maybe just knowing that can help you get your diploma and make some small plans.

Yah, but when I'm feeling so depressed it's hard to do anything.

I know. I was depressed for a long time too, and it is hard, but not impossible. Here's a technique that was given to me and was really helpful. It's called S.T.O.P. Whenever you feel desperate, like you don't belong, **STOP**. Take a breath. **Think**. **Observe** why you are feeling the way you do. Ask someone you trust if there are other ways to see the problem. **Process**, consider other options and things you can do instead. This gives you control. This helps you belong on your terms.

I like that. That's something I can do. I wish my friend had known these things.

Do it for her, and for you. Use S.T.O.P. as often as you need to. At the beginning, it felt like I was using it for every other thought I had, and slowly things began to change. And they will change for you too.

Thanks. Really. Thanks.

Blank Page Suggestion:
Write down options and things you would like to do with your life.
Make a plan. Your plan for your life.

How did i get here
i know that i am zoned out
But i can't zone in

What an awful place to find yourself in. I'm so sorry.

You don't have to zone in, not right now. Remember, it's OK.

I'm here. When you feel ready, there are some great meditation apps that can help you. When you're ready.

I'm ashamed to say it, but every day that passes makes it a little bit easier to deal with the reality of things. Simply, that he is gone. My big brother. Dead, death, gone. I'm supposed to use words like "passed on," or "gone forward," "left this earthly world"…like I could pretend pretty words filled that casket instead of you. It's difficult, especially when I also have to pretend. Pretend it's not so bad. It is. I keep thinking you might jump up out of that coffin and yell "just kidding." But you don't. I'm drinking too much whiskey, smoking too much. Seventeen and stupid I guess, thinking pain may keep you alive.

Anything but stupid, I'd say. Look at how clear you are, hating the pretending. That takes a lot of courage. I'm sorry that your brother died. It sounds like he was a great big brother. Your pain shows how much you loved him. Your pain is real. And that's OK. Right now, it feels like you are connected to him through your pain. I get that. Another option…memories. Ones that make you laugh, ones that make you grateful he was, he is, your brother. Can you find some of those, even one?

Funny, yes, I can find one. It almost hurts more, but it's a different hurt. OK, I'll look for more memories.

Good for you, one at a time, take it slow.

OK.

My cousin died a few months ago. We were a year apart and really close, like sisters, in fact. She had a reaction to an antibiotic for something, and that was it. I'm in grade 10. It happened right around exams. I feel shitty every day. And no one seems to care, like only exams seem to matter. I feel like a number in a system. I'm sad all the time and feel really alone. And because she was my cousin, I guess I wasn't supposed to be so sad. So I stopped telling anyone. They didn't understand. And then if someone said something that reminded me of her, I would just get quiet, for the whole day, and when I got home I'd just go to my room and lie on my bed. And now I just want to lie on my bed all day.

I'd want to lie on my bed too. How difficult. I'm so sorry about your cousin. It's hard to think of her right now, painful, I understand. So when you're lying on your bed, try to listen to calming or uplifting music, music that speaks to you. Music can change our mood and help us to think different thoughts. Lie on your bed as much as you need to; it's how you are healing from this traumatic event. And find some music that can slowly help to heal your heart.

I'm in grade 10 this year, first semester. Yesterday, my friend killed herself. I found out when someone sent me a text. One of our own took her life because she was so sad. She had no one to talk to. Not even me. And now I have no one to talk to. I don't know how to feel about this, like everything is in slow motion now. The principal told the school what happened on the P.A. But he never said the word "suicide." He said it was an unfortunate circumstance. No one, not one teacher, not one parent, and so not one student will say the word...suicide. She committed suicide. There, I said it. Everything is cold, and I don't know what to do. Everyone just carries on, business as usual. But nothing is usual now.

You are showing a lot of courage to do what everyone else is afraid to do. You are right. She committed suicide. There, I said it too.

Wow, it surprises me how that helps, just hearing you say the word. Thank you.

When someone dies, the world does feel cold. I remember feeling cold when someone I cared for died. I was just shivering. So I wrapped myself in a sweater and kept it close and tight to me as long as I needed it.

I have a sweatshirt she left at my house. I'll put that on and wear it. Is that a good idea?

That is a beautiful idea. And talk to her. You can always talk to her.

I like that a lot. Thanks.

We knew this day would come
But there's no way to prepare
And my thoughts are everywhere

I wanna let it all out
Maybe just scream and shout
But I have to keep it in
My walls are becoming thin

It's just my family here
But I'm trying not to shed a tear
This was my greatest fear

Oh, you are working so hard to be strong. Being there for your family. All so hard.

Grief does make things feel thin. I remember feeling like that too, when a loved one of mine died. Thin. Yes. Is there a place where you can let it all out, maybe a forest nearby or a pillow on your bed? And you can keep writing as well. Letting it out will help you feel less thin.

OK. I need to feel less thin. It's scary. I like the pillow idea. I so need to scream. OK, yes, I will keep writing. My thoughts feel less jumbled after. Thanks.

This is a hard time. Be gentle with yourself.

Orange
Moments

Orange Moment

I was in grade 9. Two days after Christmas, my mom got a call that her sister was in the ICU. We drove down to the hospital. She was already in a coma. It was scary, creepy almost. I don't know how to explain it. I felt like I was suffocating. That night in my bedroom, everything felt like it was spinning. I had to keep one foot on the ground. And my mom told me she had this dream where she thought she saw her sister standing in the door of her bedroom. The next day, in the hospital room, my mom was holding her hand. Mom's eyes were huge, like she couldn't grasp what was happening. She looked like she was six years old. I'd never seen my mom like that before; vulnerable, scared. That terrified me. And then, just like that, she stopped breathing and she died. And I just stood there, frozen, watching things go on around me. I couldn't go to my mom with my tears, I couldn't go to my dad, or my sisters. I was standing alone in this spinning room.

I don't know what to do. My mom's sister died, but it feels like my mom's gone too. What do I do?

Such a tragic event, and being around Christmas makes it so much harder. It is terrifying when we see our anchor crumble; it feels like we are just floating on our own. What you can do is be there for your mom right now. Hug her, makes sure she has food she likes and warm drinks, and just listen. That will help her heal. And she'll come back, she will.

I'm in grade 12. My dad died six months ago. He died in a hospital. We all used to watch those hospital shows, like Grey's Anatomy, but no more. I guess the memories are still thick. Sometimes it feels like they are strangling me, and it will always be like this, not being able to do things, becoming kind of paralyzed when something comes up, like a TV show. That would really suck if I'm always going to feel like this. Am I always going to feel like this?

The simple answer is no, you won't always feel like this. But right now it's like a bit of a protection for you. It's keeping you from being flooded and overwhelmed with memories. Right now they are hard to take. "Thick" is a good word for what memories can feel like right now. Sometimes, not moving is a good thing. Memories can keep us still. And you know, that's not a bad thing at all. You have had a big loss; it's like a big wound. And being still is part of healing. It's OK to be still. It's OK not to want to watch those TV shows right now.

Blank Page Suggestions:
Make a list of things that make you feel uncomfortable right now,
and another list of things that bring you small comforts.

Orange Moment

My dad died last summer. It's Christmas now. Well, that's what everyone is calling it. But every time I hear someone say it, my stomach feels a bit queasy and my chest gets all tight. We'd be putting up the lights now with Dad. It was always kind of a family affair. But there won't be any lights this year. And no tree either. None of us can do it. In fact, we're going on a cruise to the Caribbean. Anything but be here.

Oh, this is so hard. It sounds like your dad has been a huge part of your Christmas times. Your memories, full of moments with him, are hard to remember right now, they just make you hurt all over. Your whole family is hurting. What a wise decision to do something completely different this year. And it's OK. It's OK to leave those Christmas rituals until you are all ready to decide how you would like to "do" Christmas. But not this year. And maybe not next year. And one year you will want to put up the lights and the tree — just not yet. You are all doing this trip together, as a family, and that's so important.

Orange Moment

Isolation
Is anybody there?
I feel all alone.
People all around me,
Please, put down your phone.
People come and people go,
Scattered all about.
Like the waves, they ebb and flow,
If you find one, lookout!
I'm here for you they say,
Your obstacles are mine.
Call me any day,
It matters not the time.
Many days go by,
I haven't heard from you.
I have something to clarify,
I don't know what to do.
I just need a person,
Someone who shows they care.
A friend who will listen,
An answer to my prayer.

I hear your prayer.
I'm here.

I'm in grade 9. We buried my dad the other day. Well, he was cremated first, and then we buried his ashes in this tiny little box. It was wood, with this varnish on it and a stencil of a sailboat; he loved sailing. It looked like a mini coffin. I wanted to put his ashes into the lake where he loved to sail, but Mom said they had to go into this plot so people could come and visit him. I think that's plain crap, but it doesn't seem to matter what I say anyway. Other people look so mechanical when they go to their "plot," and that's what it will be like for us. But I won't go. That will just be Mom. I won't go. She can water her flowers all by herself. Dad hated flowers anyway. When I want to talk to him, I'll go and sit by the water.

Good for you. You have your special place where you can connect with your dad. That's all that matters. I love that you are standing up for yourself.

Thanks. I kinda needed to hear that.

Awesome.

Orange Moment

End of high school
New beginnings
Shattered with the death
Of my love
Drunk driver
Street corner
As the moon watched
And I slept
To wake in horror.
They are gone
My love is gone
My dreams
Taken
By the moon
And metal
And alcohol
And now
Only
Shadows.

I'm so very sorry. How awful. You lost your love. You lost your anchor, didn't you?

What do you mean my anchor?

An anchor holds us in our life; it gives us a feeling of security and safety. Were they your anchor?

Oh yes, my anchor. I never knew that word. But wow, that is so true. My anchor. My safety is gone. What do I do now?

You remember your love, and you take that power into yourself and so find a new anchor in yourself. You're not alone, and you never will be. Your love is always with you. Pull on that to keep your new anchor strong.

I love that. So perfect. Thank you so much.

I'm in grade 9. I've lost my courage, I've lost my nerve. Four months ago my dad and I were driving home from a hockey game. The roads were a bit icy. It was dark. I could smell that my dad had had a few beers, but it was always hard to tell if it was too many. He went around a corner too fast, and we went flying off the road right into a tree. It was terrifying. If we hadn't been wearing our seatbelts, we would have been dead immediately. As it was, we were still pretty banged up, and the car was totalled. I got stitches in my head from where I connected with the windshield. My dad split his head right open and broke his hand. He died later from complications. I still can't believe it. I don't remember how any of that happened. I'm terrified, I'm terrified to get in a car with anyone except Mom, and I'm terrified to tell any of my friends. It's starting to affect my work at school because I seem to be always worried that someone is going to offer me a ride home, or a ride to a game, or a ride somewhere. And I just can't do it. I'm so terrified of someone else dying from a car accident.

What a terrifying experience you went through. And to lose your dad, what a shock. You are still in shock. Getting in a car will be difficult for you, and that's OK. You can just travel with your mom for a while, that's OK. Your good friends will understand. Choose a friend that you feel safe with and tell them how you feel. That is how you begin to heal your grief and sadness. By talking. And understanding yourself. There are places on the Internet that explain PTSD. Perhaps take a look. It will help you understand some things you are feeling and experiencing. One step at a time. You'll be OK. You'll get there.

Blank Page Suggestion:
Draw a circle that represents your heart and fill in that space with
pictures that show how you feel.

I'm in grade 11. I lost my best friend. My best friend was killed in a car accident a couple of months ago. She was my friend since grade 3. We had all these plans to go to the same university and travel around Europe together, live beside each other when we got married. So many things. She was my family. My sister, really. I loved her. And now she's gone. Just like that. Gone. I guess because she was "just" my friend, people feel I should be over it all, not be sad anymore. She wasn't "just" my friend. I feel like I might crack open at any minute. And there's no one I can tell.

I'm so sorry you lost this dear friend. And I'm so sorry that you feel no one will hear you and your sadness. She was your friend/sister. Yes, I bet you feel you could crack open at any minute. Your sadness won't be over quickly. So take your time. This loss was about your relationship, and you had a significant relationship. You can tell her how you're feeling, and for now, that will help. You can write a letter to her. You can talk to her whenever you need to. She is still close to your heart. You will never lose that.

I know you feel there is no one who will understand; often that is our own fear talking. There will be a person who will understand, someone you can talk to about how this has affected you. Can you think of a close friend you can trust, or a parent or teacher? This is when you find your circle of safe people. And we all need to find that.

Blank Page Suggestion:
Write down all the people that could be in your circle of safety. Write down how you feel as a way to find your words for the moment when you will talk with someone.

I'm in grade 9. My dad has leukemia. He's been given a few weeks to live. I remember how scary it was when they told us the chemo wasn't working. I didn't know what to do with that. Then it was a yes, then it was a no. It is a roller coaster ride. And it's always in the back of my head, just knocking around. Makes it really hard to do any work at school. So I have to pretty much live two lives: one at school, and one at home. And to be quite honest, they both suck.

You are so right. They both suck. I'm sorry for the hard journey for you, your dad, and your family. It is exhausting living two lives. And that roller coaster of yes and no and yes, never really knowing what's happening. Wow. When we're on a roller coaster, we are always anticipating what's coming next, that's what makes it so crazy. Maybe instead, when you're at the top, stop, enjoy the "yes," enjoy the view, the good moment. And then when you are at the bottom, with the "no," with difficult moments, just be there and give as much comfort to your dad as possible. You're doing great, you really are.

As far as your work at school, just do what you can when you're on the top of the roller coaster. Just do what you can. OK?

Yah, OK.

Blank Page Suggestion:
Make a list of things you can do without pushing yourself too hard. Underneath, write what you will do for a break to care for yourself before doing anything else. Maybe a walk, a video game, talk with a friend. You decide. It helps to write things down. Makes it real.

Most people spend maybe a week in the hospital. We were there for about six months, hoping my dad might come home. We even brought the dog, Susie, in one day, and she went crazy when she saw Dad. He died about a week later. Dad's favourite place to sit and watch TV at home was in his La-Z-Boy chair with Susie beside him. Now Susie curls up in his chair, not wanting to eat. I think we all want to do that, curl up in his chair and not eat. Too bad the chair's not bigger. I bet we'd all just curl up in there together. It's awful with him gone. I don't know how to say it, really.

Susie seems to be saying it for all of you. Animals are like that. Maybe sit with Susie and give her lots of hugs. It will help both of you.

I'm in grade 9. It was hard when my aunt died. We were all really close, lived beside each other, and she was like another mom to me. We went to see her in the hospital, some checkup that went really bad. And she died. I still can't believe it. And when we left the hospital room, we just left, didn't cover her with a sheet or anything. It felt so wrong. And then because she was being cremated, they put her in a borrowed casket at the funeral. A borrowed casket...what is THAT? I just can't get it out of my head, just leaving her there in that hospital bed all exposed and then in a borrowed casket. I just can't get it out of my head. I just want to know she's OK, know what I mean?

Yes, I know what you mean. Your aunt was a special lady. Wanting the very best for her was and is important to you. What really bothered you?

That we just left her in that room. Kind of abandoned her, I guess. Like, I wanted to go back and at least cover her with the sheet, you know. Finish it, like a goodbye, but I didn't know how. No one else suggested it.

I can see that would feel really uncomfortable. No one knows how to do any of this "right." You can go back in your mind, if you like, recreate that moment and go and cover her with the sheet, finish it the way you wanted to. That will help.

Yah, that's actually a good idea. I'll do that. Change it in my head. OK.

Orange Moment

Who has taken the winds?
The winds that dry my tears
When they well up behind my eyes
Fighting to drag themselves to the surface
And with them
Feelings better left buried.

It's OK to stay beneath the surface, under the radar, for now, if that is what you need.

I remember when I was in grade 10, my sister was diagnosed with cancer. She was in grade 12. She came back to school once before she died, in a wheelchair, wearing a wig. She was so skinny. Everyone treated her like she would break, which I guess was kinda true. She died shortly after that visit. People in school would say lame things like "sorry for your loss" and then just go to class. Funny, all the teachers just expected me to keep up with assignments, prepare for exams. It's weird because doing assignments was the last thing on my mind. And when I was still sad after a week, I don't know, it was like I wasn't allowed to still be sad, like I was just this hormonal teenager. Someone even said to me, "Oh you're young, you'll get over it." I feel so alone because now I know I can't talk to anyone. Even my friends are so uncomfortable when I talk about it. So I'm now a robot. Just doing what everyone tells me to do. No feelings. None.

That's hard. I think you know that being a robot and having no feelings isn't helpful. You are wise enough to know that. You also know that you need to talk about your feelings — good for you! Indeed you do. Thank you for telling me how you feel.

I remember when I had a difficult loss and people around me just didn't know what to do or how to respond. It is lonely! I had to find ways to let my feelings out. My tears felt like I was talking — talking to the one I lost as well as talking to myself about how I was feeling. I didn't feel like writing, so I tried painting, and I would just let the colours flow.

Your sister was and is special to you. You will be sad for a lot longer than a week, that's for sure! Let's find ways for you to express your sadness and all the other emotions that you have as you miss her.

Like how, what ways can I express my sadness...and my anger?

Well, to answer that, I have to ask you a question first. What kinds of things do you like to do? Do you like to write, do art, music, sports?

Well, I like music.

OK, that's a good start. So we're talking about finding ways to express your sadness and anger. You know, behind your anger is more sadness. Being with your sadness will help your anger as well. Music can help you. Find songs that have hope in them. Listen and maybe read the lyrics. You may listen to one song over and over again. That's OK. It becomes your comfort song, and maybe lets you cry. And that's OK too.

I will, I will for sure. I like that idea. Thanks.

Blank Page Suggestion:
Find music that speaks to your sadness and also shows you hope.

Orange Moment

"Time heals all," they say.
Have they ever lost a parent?
The only thing time can relay
Is an extension of the pain.

Sure, I guess burdens change,
But they don't get any lighter.
We just constantly rearrange,
Stronger from carrying it so long.

A hole, a void, an emptiness unfilled,
Creates lifelong struggles
Your heart forever chilled.
Navigating uncharted waters.

Numb it out, alcohol and drugs.
The result of a teenager
Who got half the hugs.
Talk it out in therapy.

The more I grow, the harder it is to connect.
People don't understand
How hard I work for respect.
Most people have it handed to them.

Always labelled a lost cause,
Fought to prove myself.
Others never stop to pause
To think about the odds against me.

What I continually try to fathom
Is the haunting phantasm
That my identity was so shaped
The day my dad escaped
From life.

Do you feel you were labelled because no one really knew what was going on for you?

Exactly. And it just ballooned from there. I started to become what everyone said I was. But I'm not that. I don't want to be. Even now, being in university and having a goal, which is all good, and I worked hard for this...but I still struggle with who I am.

You are beginning to create yourself anew. One step at a time. You're doing a great job. Do you ever talk to your dad? Do it as much as you can. Tell him what excites you, what you love to do, what you're scared of. His answers will blend with yours, and you will begin to find your new path. How does that sound?

Different, and pretty good. I like it. My dad's been gone a long time, and I didn't really know how to make him part of my life. Now I do. Thanks.

It won't all happen tomorrow.

I know. But it is beginning.

It sure is. Your dad is proud of you.

My best friend died in a car accident in August. Then I had to go back to school in September and start grade 11 like nothing had happened. But something did happen. He was more than a friend — he was my brother, the one I looked up to. And now he's gone. I feel like an empty shell of a person. I want to tell someone how much I'm hurting, but everyone just treats me like a little kid who has lost a toy. No one gets why I am so sad over my friend dying. You know, like, because he wasn't my blood family it isn't supposed to hurt so much or something. But it does hurt. And no one cares. No one cares. But they care if I'm late for football practice.

Oh, how very difficult. It sounds like your friend was an anchor in your life, and that had nothing to do with whether he was blood-related or not. I understand that.

Your feelings are important. They show just how important that relationship was to you. I get that.

What do you need right now?

I needed that. I just needed to hear you say that. Thank you for recognizing my pain.

I do. I really do.

Blank Page Suggestion:
Make a family tree of who you see in your chosen family.

93

My moms were awesome. They were so happy together. Don't get me wrong, it wasn't easy at school all the time. People just misunderstand so many things. And then my one mom got really sick, really fast. Within months of the diagnosis, she was gone. My mom was crushed. She couldn't get out of bed for days, and I had to look after everything and go to school. We put together a small funeral. Not many came. Even my grandparents were split about coming. One came, one didn't. My moms were such incredible, loving people. Why can't others see that? Why do they have to see, I don't know, dysfunction. I had a loving home. Still do. But it's hard now, and lonely, and sad. I miss her. I'm worried for my mom. And I'm so very sad and isolated.

That must be so isolating. I'm so sorry. You have a lot on your plate right now. How is your mom doing?

Better. She is starting to go back to work. But she's just so sad. I feel like if I show my sadness it will be too much for her.

I understand that, and yet you need to feel your grief too. If you can't think of someone you can talk to about your grief and sadness, someone you trust, then get your feelings out in some other way. The key here is that you need to release those feelings. Cry loudly into a pillow, go for walks in a park or forest where you can freely cry, use the pages in this book to write to the mom you lost and tell her how you're feeling. When I suffered a huge loss in my life, I felt it really helped to create something for them.

OK, I see what you're saying. Yes, I will try to start to let my own grief out. I really like the idea of making something. My mom loved pottery, and she loved to cook.

That's wonderful. Maybe you could work with some clay or create a new recipe. What do you think?

I'm not a very good cook, but I like the idea of the clay. Maybe make a bowl, and I can keep special things, pieces of her jewellery in that.

That's a great idea. And remember those walks and cries and letter-writing. It will all be part of your grief journey.

OK, thanks. I feel less lonely already. Thanks so much.

Blank Page Suggestion:
Make a list of things you could make to celebrate the person that you
have lost. And then maybe a drawing of what you want to create.

Orange Moment

I'm in grade 10. I feel so alone since my friend died, like there's just no one to talk to. Teachers just care about what they're teaching. Everyone is interested in their own stuff. I've tried to talk to my parents, but that wasn't very successful. I'm getting so depressed. So I decided to cut myself with a blade, ease my mental pain. I did it on my upper thigh and the sides of my belly so no one would see. It did help; the pain is a distraction. A dirty secret. But at least it's mine. Then I cut too deep, and it was bleeding badly at school, so they called home. Great. Did my parents help? Nope. They just said I was dumb to do that to myself and to stop. What a joke. Cutting is the only thing that helps. Even the doctor just gave me pills to sedate me so I can sleep. They don't really work. I just won't cut so deep next time.

I'm so sorry about your friend. What a terrible loss for you.

Thanks.

I see how hard you're trying to deal with your pain. Such an awful place, such hard feelings.

Yes.

Seems like cutting yourself is your last resort, is that right?

Yah, like no one would talk with me, and I didn't know what else to do. At least the cutting stopped the painful thoughts.

I understand, a way to let things out, literally. But there is another way. Let me share that with you, OK?

Sure.

Sometimes your own pain can be relieved when you reach out to others. Perhaps consider going to a local humane society, where they take animals in, and see how you can help. Those animals are all suffering and lonely and need someone to love them, and help them. This can be another way to get your own pain out, and not by hurting yourself, but by helping another. What do you think?

My friend really loved animals too. I don't know if that will help, but I'm willing to try. I'll give it a try.

Good for you.

My nana had a heart attack at our dining room table about six months ago. She was taken to the hospital and died shorty after. I'm still in grade 10. I can't go into the dining room, no matter what my mom says. I am not doing very well at school, and I have nightmares almost every night, so I'm tired all the time. Most nights I wake up in tears, shaking, struggling to breathe and wondering what is going on. Sometimes, I was even scared to leave the house. Everyone in town seems to know what happened. They say things to me like, "You're young, dear, you'll be fine." I just listen and smile, feeling like I've just been punched in the gut. Fine? When will I be fine? The doctor gave me anti-anxiety pills. They actually make things worse. Will I ever be fine? Ever again? Feels like everything is out of control, especially me.

I remember when you told me about your nana, how you were there making tea for her and how she just seemed to slump over in her chair. I also remember how you froze in shock at what was happening. It's remarkable that you have been able to return to school after such a traumatic experience.

Can we talk a bit about trauma together? What you are experiencing, the nightmares, the shaking, the tears, hard to breathe, the fear, can all be ways that your body is telling you that you that this experience has shaken you to the core. The trauma wants to be heard. This is often called PTSD. You can find websites to help explain what PTSD is and things you can do to help yourself. Have a look, OK?

OK. Thanks.

My mom and dad divorced. I'm in grade 10 now. I'm finding it hard to concentrate, and I never found school hard before. And when I thought it couldn't get worse, my dad died in a work accident. I hadn't seen him often because he had moved so far away. I didn't get to say goodbye. I cry myself to sleep a lot, but no one knows that. It reminds of my little fish when I was little. I named him Fred, and I loved to watch him swim around in his little bowl, with these colourful rocks and fake trees. And then one morning he was floating on the top. I was crushed, and all my mom said was, "Flush him down the toilet." That's how it feels now. Like I'm just supposed to flush all my feelings down the toilet. Sometimes I wish it was that easy. Poor little Fred. I hated flushing him down the toilet. Just like I hated it when Dad died.

Divorce is a big thing, for sure. It is a huge loss. Your entire life changed. And to have that compounded with the death of your dad is tragic. I am so very, very sorry. It's OK to miss your dad and feel sad. It really is.

It sucks.

It does suck, and right now is hard. It can't all just be flushed away. I'm sorry about Fred, by the way. Our animals are so important to us.

He was important, and I never got to tell anyone that. Or about Dad.

Do you need to tell anyone something now? It's important to tell someone how you feel.

I need to tell my mom that I hate all this. But I blame her, I really do. I don't think she'll listen.

She may or she may not. People don't always listen when we want them to. Sometimes they just can't. You need to find a way to speak your mind, get it out of your head. What you could do is sit down and write out all the things you would like to say to your mom and to your dad. Maybe write a letter to your mom and give it to her; that would be a start. And write a letter to your dad as well. Get your feelings onto paper. That will help stop the things going around and around in your head. Can you try that?

OK. I'll try that.

Blank Page Suggestion:
Write out what you need to say to people.

Yellow Moments

Yellow Moment

I'm in grade 11. Nightmares of the crash follow me into my sleep. I let them rule my life still. I push my family aside. They can't fix what is broken inside me. Maybe I don't want to let go of the pain, because, well, now, it's all I have left of my brother. I'm trying, though, everyday, more and more. I am not ashamed to feel OK about losing him. And I'm not going to try to pin down my feelings with words. That doesn't work either. Actions, how I live my life, who I choose to be, that's how I want to honour him. That's my next step. I hope it's good enough for my brother.

You need never feel ashamed of your feelings. And to honour someone you have loved and lost with how you now choose to live your life...a great honour for the one who has died. Bravo.

Yellow Moment

I'm outside myself,
Watching...
She watched his first seizure,
watched him change,
Watched the tumour eat his brain.
Doctors explaining
"It's a bad thing that eats the good."

She watched him struggle,
Tried to accept his own demise.
She couldn't understand it,
"Why don't I recognize my own dad?"

She watched him shut down,
motionless in a coma.
Doctors reassuring,
"He can't speak, but he can hear."

She watched the family say goodbye,
she didn't know how to say goodbye.
Staring blankly at a stranger,
she never watched him again.

I'm still outside,
watching,
waiting.
She was ten when he died.
fifteen years later,
She still is.

If I was standing beside you, I would hug you right now. Do you
need a hug?

I've needed a hug for a long time.

I'm in grade 11 now. Two years ago, my best friend died suddenly. I had no idea how to cope with death. None at all. And there was no one to go to. It felt like I was walking around with this secret somehow. I became antisocial. I was so scared to tell anyone, especially my parents. I was scared about what would happen if I was brutally honest. If I started to cry uncontrollably. So I just did my school work and some extracurricular stuff. A lot of schoolwork. And so, I have very few people in my corner when I need someone. It's lonely. It's isolating. And yet I don't know how to get out, how to tell my secret.

Oh, you've carried this by yourself for a long time. At first it was OK, keeping it quietly to yourself and keeping busy. You're right, secrets can be isolating.

Yah. I really don't like being so lonely. But I'm still scared I will cry when I talk about it.

I get that. And that's OK. Often we are told that tears are a sign of weakness, that there is something wrong with us if we cry. Tears are a universal language, a language we are losing in our society. They are part of your language, your heart. Speak your tears as much as you need to. That will help you tell your secret, and then it won't be a secret anymore.

Oh, I really like that.

Blank Page Suggestion:
In the safety of these blank pages, consider writing out your secret.
It is a beginning to letting it go. Letting it out.

I worry about the weather
If I locked the door
If I put lunch in
My backpack.
Is homework done?
Is Mom OK?
Do my friends still like me?
When Dad died
He left me
With so much
And I worry
I won't remember
I'll forget
I'll let him down
I worry
I'll forget.

That's a lot for you to carry. You must miss him very much. You won't forget him. You won't. You're worrying a lot. That will start to impact your physical and emotional health. Let's find ways for you to reduce worrying. You seem to have a lot of responsibilities since your dad died. Perhaps use an app or a small book and record things that you need to do. If you have a phone, put reminders in, and that can help you. That way you don't have to hold so much in your head. Now you can begin to look after yourself more, focus on your schoolwork and your friends. Another suggestion would be to find a good app that could help you to meditate, to calm your mind, which really alleviates the need to worry. Maybe create a soothing playlist you can listen to. I'm sure your dad is really proud of you. You won't ever forget him.

When I was nineteen, my very dear friend decided to put a gun to his head and blow his brains out. That was almost forty years ago. I never really talked about the whole thing with anyone. There wasn't really anyone to talk with; no one who knew what to do with those foreign awful feelings. So they just sat there, like a lump. And even though all those years and days and hours and minutes and seconds have passed, I'm still nineteen when I think about it, think about him, which is often. I remember how he had called and wanted to talk with me one evening, but I was busy and said we would talk tomorrow. But we didn't get that tomorrow. He took that away from me, from us. I know he was tormented because he was transgender, tormented by it, struggling to find where he fit in himself and in such an unforgiving, unaccepting, intolerant world. I was always there for him, except for that evening. A day that hovers and never really ends. I call his mom on his birthday each year, and we cry together. He left so many behind who loved him, but in his note, it was clear that he really didn't know that. And now he'll never know. And we have to live with that. When someone chooses to take their life, they also take a piece of life from each person they leave behind who loves them, and those people never, ever get that piece of themselves back. And we can never get that person back. We can never make it right. I'm still nineteen, forty years later. Still waiting to heal.

Oh, my. You have carried this with you for so long. I'm so sorry your friend felt this was his only option. This was truly a life-altering experience for you. With no one to talk with about it, you were left to hold it yourself. How lovely that you call his mom each year, such compassion. Do you have compassion for yourself?

Some days. Some days, I still feel bad about not being there when he needed me.

So that's regret. So you wonder, if you had been able to talk with him that night, if he would still be here. Correct?

I guess that is the question.

And the answer is, we don't know. There is an unknown when we are dealing with grief. It's now about learning to live with unanswered questions, not asking "why" or "what if" anymore. And in that, you begin to let go and heal.

Let go of the "why."

Yes.

I will begin to work on that. It's time.

Yes, it is. You begin to let yourself live with mystery in a positive way.

I'm in grade 10. The funeral for my dad was no picnic. I'm glad my mom asked my opinion — that helped. We closed the casket when everyone showed up. And I wrote some things down I wanted to say, but the pastor read it, because I just couldn't. I just couldn't. After there were soooo many people at the house, some I wanted there, some I didn't. But none of it really mattered. Dad was gone. He's buried in the mausoleum with the rest of the family. Kind of creepy to see a place held for my grandpa and my mom. Hard to take. I don't really like it there, so I don't go there to talk to him. I don't go anywhere to do that, really, I just talk to him, wherever. I miss him.

Yes, I know you miss him dearly. It's all hard to take, the funeral, burial, people. I'm glad your mom asked your opinion on the funeral and that you were able to write some things that could be said about your dad. Good for you. That took a lot of courage. And you have found that you don't need to go where he is buried to be able to talk with him. That means any time, any place. He is listening, I'm sure.

I'm in grade 10. We practiced the lockdown drill a lot. Then, one day, it was for real. Thing was, it was too late. He was already inside. Inside the safe walls of our school. How do I know? Because I heard the gunshots. I've only heard a gunshot on TV or at the movies. The real thing, well, let's just say scary doesn't even come close. We were all sitting against the wall in our classroom. No one had to be told to be quiet. We were all paralyzed. It seemed like hours, days even that we sat there. Straining to hear anything outside the walls of our room. I don't know how long it was. But when those doors were opened, were unlocked, all hell broke loose. I remember blood, a lot of blood in the halls. Everyone was trying to get outside, I don't really know why, I think we were just trying to get somewhere safe. School will never feel safe again, not sure any place will. No one in my class died, but five kids were shot dead, and two teachers. A lot were wounded. I don't really know what to think, or how. It's too far outside me. All of it. It's weird. We watch all these movies about people getting killed, blood everywhere, but when it really happens…it's nothing like a movie. It's nothing like anything. Except I know nothing will ever be the same again. Nothing.

You are so right, nothing will be the same again. The safety you could take for granted was suddenly and violently stolen from you. I am so sorry you had to go through this trauma.

Yah, and it was so unexpected. None of the planning and drills made any difference. And that people died, actually were shot and died in the school, like, I don't know, that's just, just…

Just terrifying.

Terrifying. How do I get past that kind of terrifying?

I don't think you get past it, but you learn to stand around it, maybe beside it. Does that make sense?

Kind of, yah. Stand beside it. That helps me feel less terrified.

Exactly. And for now, that is all you can do. Comfort yourself, comfort others, and stand beside them.

Stand. Beside. OK. For now.

For now.

It's starting to feel exactly the same as what happened to my friend last year. She couldn't cope anymore, and she killed herself. Am I next?

I'm in grade 11. I'm losing myself in this pressure. It's all around me, and I can't breathe. My parents demand high grades, they demand I succeed on teams, my teachers push me to "reach my potential," my grandparents give me money for good marks. I have no time for anything, with all the activities and teams and jobs and and and. I have to be great at all of it. Everyone keeps talking about what comes after high school, how I have to be up there with the best, so I can get this and get that. But all I want right now is to breathe. I don't even care about two years from now, or jobs in the future. All I hear are their voices in my head all the time, nattering at me. I'm losing myself, I'm really scared. I feel like I'm falling and there's no one to catch me.

OK, let's take a deep breath together. In through your nose and out through your mouth. Count to four as you inhale, count to four as you exhale. Nice and slowly. OK? Feel the shift? You can do this any time you feel cornered or trapped or terrified or lost.

In through my nose and out through my mouth, yes, I can feel it. I need things to slow down.

Yes, let's slow things down. I'm so sorry about your friend. How awful.

Yes, it was awful. We were such good friends. And it's like she never existed. No one ever talks about her at school. But I remember her. She was brilliant but felt so pressured. She never told me how bad she was feeling. I didn't know she wanted to kill herself.

Are you telling someone how you are feeling?

Who? Who would listen? No one listened to her.

Talking to someone will help ease the pressure of losing your friend, and it will begin to ease the pressure you feel at school. There is not a quick solution, but this will help, and then things will begin to feel easier. Can you think of a teacher you could talk with? A trusted friend? You would have listened to your friend if she had confided in you. Is there someone like that for you? And try to remember that parents don't always know the best thing, but they are trying; they do love you. Perhaps write a letter to your mom or dad or both. Tell them how you are feeling about the friend you lost and how much pressure you are feeling. I think you might be surprised.

I'm afraid to do that.

It's OK to be afraid. I get that. Still, write the letter to your mom. Then decide. It will look different on paper and it will help you, give you a bit of perspective.

OK, I'll do that.

And please remember, although you loved your friend and miss her very much, her story isn't your story, doesn't have to be your story. You have the power to create your own story. Please try.

Blank Page Suggestion:
What are your goals and dreams and desires? What do you like that you are doing right now? What could you take out to relieve pressure? Put them down in these pages for you to see in black and white.

Yellow Moment

We never got a chance to say goodbye
A real goodbye
We were never given the option
I hope you're OK
I'm not sure if I am, though
I understand it's a part of life
But why?
Why now?
Why you?
I have so many questions that remain unanswered
So many feelings left unresolved
So many wounds left untreated
So many words left unsaid
So I will say a few words
to you
now
I miss you

I know you do. Your questions may take a lifetime to answer. Your few words are now and always. Words of love and longing. Very precious.

Yellow Moment

I'm in grade 11. When my grandma died, it was pretty awful. She was really special to me. But people didn't seem to get why I was sad. People were like, you're still a kid, stuff like that, and I guess that meant my grief didn't have meaning. They'd just kinda poo-poo me when I said anything, you know, 'cause I haven't been around as a long as adults. I guess they think we're kinda stupid or something. We're not. "You're young, you'll get over it" makes me mad. We're being silenced. We're just not taken seriously at all. Pretty messed up if you ask me.

That would make me mad too. There does need to be a greater credibility given to young people and how they feel. I totally agree.

Thanks, I know you do, that's why I told you.

Thank you. I'm honoured.

I thought it would be different in grade 9. But the bullying didn't stop. My friend got it the worst. Why does a bully bully? One day he took my friend's backpack and dumped it all over the hall and then pushed him into a locker. He was late for class and sent to the office, and when he tried to explain why, he was told not to worry about it. Not to worry about it. What kind of answer was that? I was scared to go to school after that too. The bullying continued on social media. The Facebook posts were disgusting. And then my friend didn't show up for school. When I called his cell there was no answer. I didn't know what to do. I really didn't think he would kill himself over all of this, but I guess it just got to be too much for him. I guess he felt he had no way out but that. Now, I'm really scared.

How horrible for you. For him. For everyone. How horrible.

It was. It all was. I didn't know what to do. I didn't know how to help. I didn't want to be the next target. It makes me feel so useless. There's so much pain inside me.

Yes, I hear that. Pain of losing your friend, and your fear of that bully.

I hate that the fear of that bully is almost bigger than the death of my friend, but it is. That bully took my friend's life. He did. And he doesn't even seem sorry.

That's awful. The bully has taken so much. Don't let them take away your right to grieve and be sad for the friend you lost. Let's not let the bully keep winning. This is the time you need to talk with your parents and tell them how you are feeling. Get their help and ideas. They will be able to help you. Trust them.

Really?

Yes.

Blank Page Suggestion:
Write a note to you friend that you lost.

Blank Pages for Your Story

Blank Pages for Your Story

Blank Pages for Your Story

Blank Pages for Your Story

Blank Pages for Your Story

Green
Moments

I'm in grade 11. My dad died last year. It was just the other day that I actually was aware of my feet touching the ground. Weird. All of a sudden, I seem to be noticing things. Remembering things. Like I've been asleep a whole year or something. My dad loved music. I'm remembering that. But I haven't listened to any music for a long time. Actually, I don't remember when I last listened to anything. It might have been playing in the background, but I didn't notice background or foreground or my ground or any ground. I have this memory that pops into my head often these last few days, around the time when I noticed my feet on the ground. I remember dancing around the kitchen with Dad. He'd be singing the song that was playing on the radio, and he would twirl me and then wiggle with me and twirl me again. And we'd laugh and laugh. It makes me laugh just thinking about it. It's nice to laugh when I think about Dad.

I bet. That is such a beautiful memory. I'm so glad your feet are on the ground again. How good to finally feel grounded. Think you're ready to listen to your music again?

I think so. Maybe. Little scared.

Why?

I don't know. I think I'm scared to cry, you know, because it will remind me of dad.

But maybe you'll smile. Or maybe you'll cry. Either way, it's all good. It really is. Remember, it's OK. I think you're ready to give it a try.

Really?

Yup.

I'm in high school. My dad died about a year ago. I miss him every day, wish he was here to help me. He really was my best friend. Sometimes I worry I'll forget him. I worry about a lot of things. I try to fight it off, but it's hard. I'll think of my dad, and then I panic and try to think of the last time I thought about him...and I can't remember. And that scares me. It really scares me. I don't want to forget him, ever.

You won't forget him. I promise. Sometimes worrying we will forget actually makes the memories more fuzzy. It looks like your thoughts can take control, and not in a way that is helpful.

Yah, that's exactly it. I hate it. What can I do?

One thing you can do is give your "worry thoughts" a name, whatever the worry is. For instance, you can call them Fred, but whatever name you like. Then when the worry starts taking control, just stop and speak to it directly, by name. Say something like "OK, Fred, I hear you, but that's enough. Back off." Give it a try. See how it can work for you.

OK, that sounds like something I can do. I'll try. Thanks.

Blank Page Suggestion:
Write down all your worries here and the name you give to your worry.

141

My brother died of an overdose a few years ago. It was really hard going for a while. My pain, but also watching the pain in my parents and my siblings. But things are getting better. I'm not sure my parents will ever be the same again, not sure any of us will, but we've started to come together as a family, bit by bit. I started wearing one of my brother's sweatshirts, like you suggested. And then so were my brother and sister and my mom. For a while there, we didn't wear anything else. My aunt would come over and make us put them in the laundry. It seems kind of funny now. I still keep that sweatshirt close by, but I don't have to wear it all the time anymore. And watching that TV show my brother loved, How I Met Your Mother, was the only way I could get to sleep for months. I think whenever I'm in a stressful situation again, it will be that show I put on. I still regret that I couldn't fix what was bugging him, help him make a different choice. I still feel like I wasn't there for him when he really needed someone. And I guess I'm still a bit angry, because he took away our chance to make things better, make things right when he died.

Yes, he did do that. He did take away any chance to fix things, understand things. I can totally see why you would feel angry. I would too. You're right, he doesn't have a do-over. But you do. You are the one left behind. You have a unique wisdom now. Can you allow yourself to let go of your guilt? Because truly, no one knows exactly what would have happened, could have happened, all those what-ifs. We don't know.

That's true. There are a lot of "what-ifs." I never thought of it like that. And yah, I am left behind. I wish he knew how hard it is to be left behind. OK, so what you're saying is that I need to let the what-ifs go, is that correct?

Yes, correct. Hold on to the laughter you had together, hold on to how much you care for him, hold on to your brother and your love... but the what-ifs, that's when you need to push the delete button.

The delete button. Got it!! You know what? I hear my brother laughing. He would have loved that. Thanks.

I'm so glad you can laugh now with your brother.

Me too.

Green Moment

Now and again
We kiss memories
Of those we loved
Now and again.

Yes, now and again we do get to kiss those memories. Precious.

I'm in grade 11 now, well, almost finished. When my friend died, my world just fell apart. I cut myself, I tried to kill myself. It was pretty bad. And then one day after I took a shower, I just stood and looked at myself in the mirror. It was like this person I didn't know. She looked so sad and had these welts and red marks all over her body. At that moment, I felt really sad for her, for me. I didn't want to hurt her anymore. I'm not a mean person, and it just felt wrong to be hurting someone like that...hurting myself like that. I did go and volunteer at an animal shelter, like you suggested. They all felt sad, like I was feeling. And it did start to shift my thinking. It also started me looking at what I was actually thinking. When I started really noticing my thoughts, I realized they were pretty dark, pretty bad, not helpful at all.

I'm glad the animal shelter helped. Good for you for going there. I'm sure you've made a big difference to them. Understanding how powerful thoughts can be is really insightful. One way you can do that is to begin to understand how to talk to yourself...self-talk. Do you know about that?

Not really.

OK, well it's becoming aware of the things you say to yourself in your head. One technique is to wear an elastic band on your wrist. Each time you notice yourself beginning to think a dark thought, snap the band, and when you feel the snap it is a reminder to you, that you want a bright thought, not a dark one. And right there, change your thought. Don't take another step until you've altered that thought.

OK, and I do that every time?

Yes, every time. You will find it will get easier. And soon you will be thinking more positive and less dark thoughts right off the bat.

OK, that's great. I'll try that.

Will you keep working with the animals?

Yah, they really help me.

And what about the girl in the mirror?

I smile more at her these days.

Excellent.

Blank Page Suggestion:
Make a list of negative things you say to yourself, and then beside
each one write the opposite thought, the positive one.

My grandpa came to visit about a month ago. He doesn't come often because he lives pretty far away. He hardly came at all after my dad died. I'm in grade 12 now. Guess it's been about two years since he died. Gramps always says how much I look like my dad when he was my age. I like that; it makes me feel like Dad is close by. Gramps asked if I wanted to go for a drive one day, and when I went to get into the passenger side, he stopped me.

"You drive," he said.

"I don't know how," I answered.

"You will after today, get in."

And that's how I learned to drive. I don't know if Mom called him, or maybe Dad did. But having Gramps teach me to drive, well, honestly, it was like Dad was in the car too. It all kinda choked me up. Things about Dad always choke me up. I wish Gramps lived closer.

Yeah, Gramps! You know, he was grieving too when your dad died. That was his son, and I suspect it was just so hard to come and see you, see how much you reminded him of his son, that it took a while before he could visit. And when he did, he gave you something incredible. Gramps would have taught your dad how to drive too. What a special moment for the two of you. It's OK to get choked up. Special memories can do that. When you are ready, you can drive to visit your gramps! He'd love that. And so would your dad.

And so will I.

It's been a year since the car crash where my friends died and I walked away. I'm almost finished grade 12. Not really sure what's next. I haven't done very well this year. Sort of lost my way and failed a lot of assignments. I don't know, nothing really seems to matter. It's all over so quickly, so what's the point? But I did stop drinking. I can never get into a car again under the influence. I'm the most popular guy at every party now, because I am always the safe ride home. And I always will be. At least I can do that for my friends who didn't have a DD. Every drive home is for them. Maybe for the rest of my life. It's the least I can do.

Good for you for finding something that you can do to make a difference. Your friends would be proud of you. Such a traumatic event. It sounds like you are still suffering from PTSD. I am so sorry things are still so difficult for you.

PTSD can stick with us for a long, long time until we learn how to handle it. Then you will find your direction.

You are looking after everyone else at the end of a party. Now it's time to look after yourself.

How do I do that?

Well, first, speak kindly about yourself. This wasn't your fault. Do things that make you happy and allow yourself to enjoy it. You will heal. Keep reading this book, you will find more advice to help yourself on this journey.

I don't like this journey.

I know you don't. I don't either. Remember, it's OK. And remember, journeys go places. This is a journey of healing.

Healing. I hope so.

Remember, it's OK.

OK.

Blank Page Suggestion:
Make a list of things you like to do, things that will make you smile,
be fun. It's OK to have fun.

Green Moment

I have a feeling of peace,
The negative feelings have passed.
My mind is at ease,
At long last.
Just wait a minute,
The fear is sneaking up on me.
I have experienced quite a fright,
Please don't leave me be.
The time has finally come,
I can finally see the light.
To a smile I succumb,
Everything will be alright.

Yes, yes it will. Good for you. I'm smiling too.

Green Moment

My grandma was my best friend. She was the only one that really listened to me. She died shortly after my parents divorced, and my world crashed. I was in grade 10. I started smoking and doing drugs. I mean, it helped, you know? Kept me numb, and when I couldn't feel, at least I could do things, do school. I was high pretty much every day I was at school. Then I started binge drinking too. I felt pretty shitty all the time. Somehow, I managed to get into college. I'm starting next month. I've stopped smoking, and I don't drink like I used to. I was never addicted, you know. I needed friends, and they all did it too. Yah, getting out is hard. And just when I'm doing better and some friends ask me out, I slip back into those habits again. But I want to do well in college. I'm trying to be the master of my own life. I don't want to just survive anymore. I'm trying to do more than survive. But those habits are deep, really deep, and I'm afraid I'll never get out. Not completely. How do I do this?

Good for you for pulling yourself out of that deep hole. You had a lot of loss all at once. Now you are in a different place; you've chosen that. Good for you. Slipping back into old habits is easy. Try not to be too hard on yourself. Let me explain what's happening to you. When you find yourself in an old familiar situation, your brain and your thoughts immediately go back to how you used to think, and then your old feelings follow close behind, as do your actions. So what you need to do is recognize that initial thought. Recognize the old thought. Question it before it takes hold. Get evidence. Is the thought correct? Do you need to do the same things? Do you have a choice? Yes, you do. Once your thought changes, so will your feelings, and so will your actions. Do you see that?

Oh, for sure, you're exactly right. So I collect evidence rather than just acting on a thought.

Exactly. And come to a party prepared. Bring pop or other drinks you like that aren't alcoholic, so you have options. And if you're out somewhere and you only want one or two drinks, any pop with a piece of lime in it fits in. Slowly, you'll change those old habits permanently.

Wow, that's fantastic. Thanks so much.

Blank Page Suggestion:
Write down some thoughts or habits that keep popping up, ones that you don't want anymore. Slowly remove them from your life one by one.

Tragedy hit our high school when a grade 10 boy was killed in a gang fight. Knife wound. Two others are in critical care in the hospital. Know what makes me really sick to my stomach? That some people on social media see it as a time to promote themselves. Sure, they go on social media and post how great the person was, how much they are missed blah blah blah. But they didn't even really know them; they're just using it as a way to pump themselves up, get some attention, self-promotion. Pretty sick, really. I mean, why can't social media be the place we all try to deal with this, figure it out, so it won't happen again? If technology and social media is so amazing, why does it just seem wrong? It's all just so messed-up.

Yes, I can see how this is so sickening. Were you hoping for some help through social media? That was a traumatic event at your school. What did you need?

I guess I needed people to actually talk about the event. How people are feeling. Like I am scared now. Is anyone else scared? That kind of thing, you know?

I am sure you are scared. I'd be scared too. It's scary. Would you feel comfortable starting a blog yourself?

That's a good idea. Let me think about that.

Blank Page Suggestion:
Write down different ways you can reach out through social media to start talking about how everyone is feeling.

Turquoise
Moments

I'm in grade 11. My parents divorced when I was in grade 9, and my dad died shortly after. It was awful. It still isn't great. It's better, but it isn't great. Mom has a boyfriend now. I was sitting on the couch this Christmas watching everyone, seeing all these empty boxes in the corner, waiting to be flattened and taken out to the garbage. And I remembered something you said about having a choice about what we feel, that it is up to us. And sitting there, I didn't want to feel crappy and sad and angry anymore. And if that was truly up to me, then I want to figure out how to do that. And I wondered what it would be like to just put these rough, hard feelings into those boxes, and they could go to the garbage too. I don't want to feel shitty anymore, I just don't.

Good for you! That takes a lot of focus and intention to be able to choose how you feel about something. I'm proud of you!
  Merry Boxing Day.

A girl in my grade 10 class killed herself last week. She actually did it. We couldn't believe it. She talked about doing it, but we all do sometimes. And then she was dead. We were all in shock. She wasn't really my close friend, but she was a classmate. She was part of my world. So it was hard. But what made it worse is the silence in the school, silence in the staff. They said a student died, an unfortunate circumstance. But no one would say that she committed suicide. Like it's a dirty word or something. Thing is, the more we talk about this stuff, like really talk about it, the more we move, but if we're never actually saying what really happened, how do we move at all? Talking about it helps. I'm lucky, I can talk to my mom. But at school, it was all about the work, the assignments, the exams, the teams. If other kids don't have moms like mine, and I know lots don't, then they would just have their feelings bottled up like forever. The staff's favourite thing to say is that routine is good, helps you move on. But that's not true. It's a distraction. The bottled feelings are still bottled. Looks like a vicious cycle to me. When will it stop? When will we be brave enough to really talk, to really move and so unbottle those feelings once and for all? When?

Thank you for that. You are teaching me. I love it. When? The moment people stop being afraid of grief. And I think you are doing that right now. Thank you.

I'm in grade 12, just beginning. I'm doing much better since my friend committed suicide. It isn't uncommon for kids to feel overwhelmed with pressure. I noticed someone else struggling, so I told her about the breathing and thinking about what she really wanted for herself, things you suggested. She thought that was pretty cool. She doesn't feel so desperate anymore. That made me feel pretty good. Like I made something good out of the death of my friend. I've figured out how to breathe when I'm stressed, think about what I need. And I've been accepted at the college I want to go to. I'm OK. I'm really OK.

Wow. That's fantastic. So wonderful you were able to help someone else and feel like you honoured your friend in the process. How powerful for you. Congratulations on being accepted at a college. You have lots of tools to be successful. You can do it. Keep breathing.

I plan to. Thanks so much. Thanks for being there.

I remember when Mom died, and for months after all we did was order take-out and eat off paper plates with plastic forks. After a year, I got pretty tired of that. So one day I pulled down one of mom's favourite cookbooks and turned to the page most tattered and worn. It was the recipe for shepherd's pie. There were all sorts of notes written on the page beside, above, and below the recipe — Mom's handwriting. Tears sprang to my eyes, and I let my finger trace on top of the letters she had made. Shepherd's pie was one of her favourites. So I made a list of all the ingredients, especially her additions, and walked over to the grocery store. That night, for the first time, I attempted to make her shepherd's pie. I even set the table with real plates and metal forks and knives. Everyone sat at the table, almost like old times, I even set a place for Mom. No, it wasn't as good as Mom's at all, but it was edible, and we weren't eating take-out on paper plates, Dad actually got out of his chair, and I saw my brother. So all in all, it was pretty awesome. Now I'm looking for a recipe to cook tomorrow. For Mom.

Look at you. You found your way. Your mom is so proud.

Woohoo!!

My dad was an alcoholic and died in a car accident. I didn't know how to tell anyone. I was so embarrassed and yet so sad. I've kept the secret so long that he was drunk when he died. I started thinking I was the only one. Someone told me to go to Alateen, a place that helps teens with parents who are or were alcoholic. I couldn't believe the relief I felt. I could finally tell my secret in a safe place. So I started telling other people here and there, just when a moment came up. And more and more, I realized I wasn't alone at all. Made me wish I had told my secret long ago. I kept people so far away, I didn't really have any friends. But that is all different now. Not holding a secret, I can't believe how good it feels.

YES!!! How brave and bold. What a powerful discovery. Yes, secrets can be a poison. So glad you've found your way, and maybe you can now grieve your dad in the safety of your new friends.

Yes, I am starting to do just that. Thank you so much.

I'm proud of you.

Blank Page Suggestion:
What secrets are you keeping that need to be set free, so you can be set free? Write them down here first if that feels better. Just get them out.

Turquoise Moment

I needed to be held,
I needed someone to hear me,
For life was coming down
And I had no time to drown
You walked in on a time that was pure
And reminded me that you were sure,
Pain was OK to feel
We mustn't run
You told me that I was not done
For it's OK to stumble
for words may fumble
But grief is OK
Thus, when the days are long
I am reminded that I can go on
For you are my saving grace
Thank you
For being there
Just being there

I'm here, just here. You are so brave.

I'm going to university next year. Dad's been gone about year, well one year in four days. I talk to him a lot, well, in my head. Not out loud. He was so funny, you know. Like he watched the movie Avatar, I don't know, maybe sixty times. Whenever we would get a new TV or sound system, you know, stuff like that, he would put that movie on to test out the new TV or new system. He wanted to see if the graphics were as good on the new equipment or the sound. He wanted to see how cool the avatar looked. Then he'd just sit down, and watch the whole thing. He was funny. Who knows, maybe that's how I'll test my new TV and sound system, when I get one. LOL

What a fun memory of your dad. So nice for you to be able to laugh when you think of him now. There was a time when that would have seemed like an impossible thing to do.

So true, it is nice to laugh. I didn't think it would be possible a year ago. Still miss him, though.

Laughing and enjoying some memories doesn't mean that you have stopped missing him. It means that now you can take him with you, and have a lighter heart. That's a good thing.

Yah, you're right, it is a good thing. It really is. Thanks.

I wonder what movie you will pick to test your new TV! LOL

Ha!! Me too!!

I remember when we had to put down Tabby, our cat. She was really sick. I was in grade 9. That cat was more like a dog, really. She was so cool and such great company, especially when I was feeling sad, you know, having a really bad day. She'd curl up beside me, no matter where I was, sort of like giving me a hug. She'd follow me around the house, even into the bathroom. She liked to play with the bubbles with her paw while I was having a bath. Taking her to the vet was awful. Holding her in my arms, and then the needle and she went all limp and everything. I handed her to my mom, tears screaming down my cheeks, and she wrapped her in a blanket. We had a place we were going to bury her in the backyard, with a special stone to mark the place. I was so sad. I didn't think I'd ever recover. My mom could see when I was sad, and she'd just give me hugs, didn't say anything, just hugged me, which was so good because I had no words. And then one morning, about six months later, I came down to breakfast and there was this box beside my cereal bowl. "Take the lid off," my mom said, busy making coffee. When I opened the lid, there was little fluffball inside. She wasn't the same colour as Tabby at all, but she was so cute. I picked her up and held her close to my face, and she bit my nose, and it looked like she was smiling afterward. I laughed out loud. TomBoy, I called her TomBoy. I told Tabby all about her. I'll never forget Tabby, never. But I'm glad TomBoy is here. I really am.

That was so nice that your mom understood your sadness. How special for you. And then to have a fluffball beside your breakfast one morning. TomBoy is very lucky. So are you.

Yah, I think so too.

I'm in grade 12 now. It's been a few years since my nana died. It was all pretty traumatic, because truth be told, she died at the dining room table that night, not in the hospital. I think they told me that because they thought it would help. But I'm not stupid. I knew. I read all the articles you suggested on PTSD. Yup, that's what I had...what I have, because it seems that once that switch gets flipped, it takes a while to flip it back. I'm a lot better. Not so many panic attacks. Your words and support were so helpful when I didn't think anyone was listening. It gave me the courage to go and talk to a therapist, and she's helped me recover from the PTSD. It just went faster, smoother with someone to help me along. I know I'll be OK now, but it is a lot of work. Again, thanks for being there.

I'm so glad you had the courage to read those links provided, and to go and get help from a person. Good for you. Yes, recovering from PTSD will take time. Small, solid steps. It isn't like ripping the Band-Aid off — it's healing from major heart surgery.

Yah, that's a good analogy. It is hard, but it's also so worthwhile. It's nice to have my mind back and not be so at the mercy of those anxiety and panic attacks. I have my life back.

And you'll do great things.

Thanks. Thanks for everything.

Turquoise Moment

My dad died just as I was starting grade 12. I got through the year. I wear the chain around my neck that he always wore, it helps, it really does. Sort of like he's close by. I can't really imagine a day I'll ever take it off now. And I got his car. He was all about the car. The car. I will keep that car in good shape and drive it like he liked to drive...fast and free. I'm off to university next year, I'm OK, not super duper, but OK. But I'm worried about leaving my mom alone. It's been hard on her. I worry about her.

It sure has been hard work for you. Congratulations on graduating and on finding your way to university! I am sure your dad would be very proud of you. I suspect that chain will be a forever keepsake for you, and having his car and remembering how he loved to drive, well, that's very special.

Your mom's loss is hard. Your loss is hard. As you have found ways that work for you, she will also find ways that work for her. She knows you are there for her and care for her, even if you are away at university. I suspect she is very proud of you as well. Finding new ways to keep connected, like video chat on some kind of regular basis, will be good for both of you. You have a strong connection already. It's about finding new ways to "be together."

Turquoise Moment

I can still see you smiling
I can still see you dancing
I can still hear your favourite song
I can still hear your excitement over sports
I can still smell your cooking
I can see you
A spirit in my mind to remind me how precious life is
A spirit in my mind to remind me
of you
and all the happiness
you brought to the world
The spirit of you

Mmmmm.
   A beautiful spirit.
   Beautiful.

Turquoise Moment

He lives forever in our hearts
Even though he must depart
Although he is leaving
His lessons stay breathing
It's been almost a year
And sometimes I still feel the tears
But when I think of my father I am not sad
I am not mad
I am glad
For what he taught me
And the memories
we share

How beautiful. You have found a way to anchor your dad in your heart, and he will always be with you.

Pale Blue
Moments

Pale Blue Moment

I'm in my first year of university now. My mom died when I was in grade 11. I remember how awful it was to watch movies and TV shows that had parents in them that died, moms especially. I was always a little nervous when someone would ask me to go and see a movie with them, or when friends were having a movie night. I didn't really want to have a panic attack around them. And then one night I was pretty tired, and I just put a movie on, not thinking. Turned out it did have parents in it that died. But I didn't have a panic attack. I had a gratitude attack.

That's what I'm calling it anyway. Sure, I was crying, but I was smiling too. Because it hit me that I was pretty lucky to have such a great mom. And even though I miss her every day, I now know I can watch movies and not fall apart when a parent dies. I can smile and feel gratitude.

Oh, I love that phrase, gratitude attack! And what a journey it has been for you to get here! Sure, it didn't happen all at once, but you gave yourself space for those triggers, you were kind to yourself, and you slowly worked your way to the place you are today. Good for you! Triggers will come, truly for the rest of your life, some happy, some sad. You know that now. And you have a way to move through them and even find your mom in them. And those tears, well, sometimes I call mine happy/sad tears. They can both exist at the same time.

You've learned a lot, grown a lot. Well done.

When my cousin died a few years ago, I didn't think I would ever get rid of that pain. A pain that just took over my whole body and mind. I did what you said, though. While I was lying on my bed, I started to listen to uplifting music or music that spoke to me. I began to make a new playlist and listened to it whenever I started feeling low and deeply sad. It got me through. You were right, music does help to shift mood and thoughts we think. I'll never forget that. Thank you so much.

Wonderful. I'm so glad you have found something that can give you your power back. That took courage. Good for you.

In grade 11, my dad finally got custody of me, after my mother died of an overdose. I started at a new school. I was pretty timid and insecure, but soon my grades were good Bs and a few Cs, and I stopped hanging out with the kids on the corner. I'm not as depressed as I used to be. I have a goal now to be a social worker and help kids in bad places. So, school is more important. I'm doing another year of high school, fifth year, and lots of online courses to try to catch up, get my marks up. I used to believe all the awful things my mother said about me, said to me, but more and more I realize she was not a very nice person. I am a nice person. I took your advice and started using S.T.O.P. when my thoughts got the best of me. It really helped and became a good habit. I still use it now when I feel my thoughts going in a bad direction. Life is pretty good right now.

Such a great place to be. That's so great to hear. I remember when we talked about S.T.O.P. and about making a plan for yourself. How brave you are, working to create new habits and become mindful of your thoughts. Such empowerment. Sounds like you have created a great plan for yourself. I'm so proud of you.

Thanks. That means a lot to me. Thanks for being there when I really needed someone.

I'm glad I was there for you, though the reality is you chose to be there for yourself. Bravo.

Thanks. That makes me smile.

It's been a couple of years since Dad died. I think the first Christmas we needed to run away, so we went on a cruise. The next year we stayed home but didn't do too much. This year I don't think we'll put up any lights outside, but I'm ready to have a tree again. Dad really liked it. He'd sit in his spot on the couch with a beer and just watch us all fussing about, decorating the tree. He had this really big laugh. I remember it a lot at Christmas. His chair is still empty, but he's there. I feel him. And I want to do the tree for him, remember him, you know? It's weird, when someone dies, someone you really love, it's like you're split. Split between living in the world of memories and living in the world in front of you. I don't know if they ever connect, but at least I'm getting better at living in them both and not being so sad all the time.

I remember what you told me about your first Christmas, how hard it was to have the memories. They made you ache all over. You and your family took your time to find your way with how to "do" Christmas, and now this year, your memories are bringing you comfort and even joy. Wow. How sweet is that?

I like how you put it, like being split and living in two worlds. I guess we could say that the world in front of you brings the invitation for the memories, finding comfort and stories that make this world richer, in a way.

I'm proud of you.

Pale Blue Moment

When my parents both died in an accident, my world ended. Just stopped. I didn't know if I could even go to university. I had to move in with my aunt. She lived just outside of town, and there was this huge forest behind her house. I remember I started to go into the forest when I'd come home from school or my summer job. Sometimes I would just hug a tree and cry. Sometimes I would sit with a book, leaning against a tree. Sometimes I would pull bark off the tree and scream. Sometimes I would lie on the ground and look up through the leaves to the tip-top branches, clouds floating above. The trees were there for me somehow. It was like they were giving me strength and space and comfort. I could think about my mom and dad there, and it was OK. And slowly I realized that what I had wanted to do was protect these places. These places, these trees that were now protecting me. I did go to live in residence. But I didn't start until second semester. I did wait, like you suggested. It was a good idea. Otherwise, I wouldn't have found the trees, and I don't think I would have found myself. I'm in second year now. It's still painful not having my parents. But as weird as it might sound, it's like they were talking to me through the trees. There are some great parks close to this university, and I often go there, just to sit with the trees...sit with Mom and Dad. I guess as long as there are trees, I'll feel Mom and Dad close. I'll feel safe.

So I have to look after them. That's my direction now.

Wow, you have done a lot of hard work since your parents died. I'm so proud of you. You found a safe place of comfort to feel the loss of your parents. What a beautiful image that the trees were there for you. You found your passion again, and it ended up being in the direction you were planning, but now it is yours with new energy and personal connection. As long as there are trees, you will feel your mom and dad close. Thank you for those beautiful words and that beautiful image. Bravo.

Pale Blue Moment

The world is spinning
Fast
And sometimes
Out of control.
People come
And people go.
There for you one minute
Not the next.
But I can sit on the center
And watch the world
Spin all around me
Watch others spinning
Without spinning myself.
I am my own strength.
I alone hold my balance
In the palm of my hand
In the chaos
I am my own peace
I am my own anchor.

That's a powerful place to sit when you can be your own anchor.
Bravo!

I'm just finishing high school. My dad died halfway through. I didn't know if I'd get through it. My thoughts were going crazy, and I couldn't think straight. You suggested that I personify my thoughts, give them a name and speak directly to them. So I tried it. It was amazing. It's the only thing that helped me. And I got pretty good at it. Controlling my thoughts was huge for me. It gave me relief. Gave me control back. They weren't consuming me anymore. I wouldn't let them. I've learned how to control my emotions better too. I can take worries and thoughts and set them aside and deal with them when I want to. Cut them off when I've had enough. I call them Phil. Sometimes I listen to Phil, sometimes I don't. It's my choice. Thanks so much. I don't know what I would have done without that advice. I'm really grateful.

I'm so glad you found that helpful. That's a huge accomplishment for you! I like how you said, sometimes you listen and sometimes you don't, knowing when it's time and when you have had enough. Wow. So cool! Good for you!!!

I'm in grade 12. My dad died about a year ago. It still feels pretty sad, I don't know. Just sad. I was wishing there was some way I could talk to him, then a cool thing happened. I was walking home from school, and I saw a hawk circling around. And I remembered when my dad was alive, how a friend of ours had saved a hawk and nurtured it back to health and then set it free. My dad thought that was cool. And any time he saw a hawk, he'd say it was the same one coming to say hi. I remember him saying that if he ever died, he wanted to come back as a hawk. I looked up at the hawk and wondered. Then a couple of weeks later I was fixing something outside for my mom, and I heard this voice in my head that said I should put on safety glasses. My dad was always big on safety. And when I looked up, I saw a hawk. It's him, I know it is. Watching over us. And all of a sudden, I could take this deep breath.

Wow, that has brought tears to my eyes. What a beautiful story. Yes, he's watching. So cool.

Pale Blue Moment

I needed to be held,
I needed someone to hear me,
For life was coming down
And I had no time to drown
You walked in on a time that was pure
And reminded me that you were sure,
Pain was OK to feel
We mustn't run
You told me that I was not done
For it's OK to stumble
for words may fumble
But grief is OK
Thus, when the days are long
I am reminded that I can go on
For you are my saving grace
Thank you
For being there
Just being there

Oh, my. What a beautiful poem. What a beautiful thought. Thank you for sharing this. It's really wonderful.

I'm in grade 12. When my mom died, she left us all a letter she wrote. Her handwriting was pretty wobbly, because she was pretty sick. But it was her all over the page. I read that letter often. In many ways, it got me through the rest of high school. I made a decision the other day: I got a tattoo on the inside of my forearm. What did I put? Well in that letter my mom wrote to me she said "no one said life would be fair, but it can be so beautiful." I keep looking for the beautiful, even though it often feels pretty unfair. My tattoo says "no one said life would be fair." My mom is with me wherever I go, in more ways than one. I try to look for the beautiful, in between the unfair. Love you, Mom.

What a powerful and strong gift in those words! Your mom is indeed with you wherever you go. Beautiful.

Pale Blue Moment

I thought about you today
When the sun rose and set fire to the sky
And the moon laughed, sitting idly by
I thought you'd like to hear that
And maybe this too;
I laughed along
With the dancing winds
And smiled as well
Remembering you
Brother.

Beautiful laughter. Remembering.

I'm in second-year university. My best friend died in an accident on the water at her cottage when I was in high school. I wish I'd had someone to talk to about it, someone who would just listen, not try to fix it, because well, there really was no way to fix it. I did a lot of the suggestions you've made here over the years, and they really, really helped me a lot. It's such a raw, lonely journey, this grief stuff. I want to be able to help someone else, like you've helped me. Pass it forward kind of thing. I won't be afraid of someone's grief anymore. You've helped me see things differently. When it comes up, I'll be ready, ready to be there, quietly, with an ear, a hug, and when the time is right, some of these coping skills you've taught me. Thanks, thanks for being there. Thanks so much.

It's been my honour to be with you on your journey. You have worked hard. I know you will make a difference in someone's journey. Remember, it's important that when you help someone, you stay kind to yourself. All those coping tools you want to share are the same ones you will continue to use throughout your life.

You go, girl.

Pale Blue Moment

It's been two years since my sister died. I'm in grade 12 now. She died of cancer. In two years, I really didn't talk to many people about how I felt. I listened to music, like you suggested, and it really got me through some dark days, gave me hope just like you said. It helped make my sister feel closer. No one else either cared or knew what to do or say. It was OK, though. I was slowly figuring it out. Thing is, I still feel like I have this hole inside me. I've applied to university next year. I worked hard in school, for her. I want to work in cancer research. I'm starting with a B.Sc., and then I'll see. But I want to know more about the disease and help people and their families who suffer. Maybe along the way, I'll find some healing myself. Maybe. I miss her. I still miss her.

You are healing. Keep using your music and holding your sister close.

What a fabulous way to honour your sister's journey and death. You are finding ways to turn your experience and pain into something that may help others. That takes a lot of courage and strength! Bravo. And it sounds like you have done most of your grief journey alone. I am sad about that. I would love to hear stories about you and your sister.

That hole that you still feel, well, I guess you could say it makes sense that it is still there. How could it not be? It's like the hole is still there, and you are making the space around the hole wider and bigger, more space for you to walk on, live in. Your sister has left a hole in your life. But maybe it's not a bottomless hole, but rather a hole that collects and holds all your memories together. Reminds you of your love.

Oh wow, that just shifts it all. The hole is something I can cherish now. Thank you. I am healing. I want to heal.

You are.

Blank Page Suggestion:
Write down some memories you have of you and your loved one.

Dedicated to a lost loved one

Light
(A song by musician Niina Rosa, gifted to *Remember, It's OK*)

Saw your spirit float away
Nothing's ever gonna be the same
I don't know how to
Communicate
Communicate

I think we got it all wrong
Had our eyes closed all along
But that's why we gotta have faith

Don't be scared
Don't let 'em keep you blind
Just follow the light
Just follow the light

Thought I lost something
Thought I had nothing
Then I realized it's all inside
No one can take this away
No one can take this from you

For a while I was runnin'
Scared of myself yeah
For a while I was hopin'
Someone would tell me what to do

I think we got it all wrong
Had our eyes closed all along
But that's why we gotta have faith

Don't be scared
Don't let 'em keep you blind
Just follow the light
Just follow the light

Blank Pages for Your Story

Blank Pages for Your Story

MarinaLRead
↑
Talker
Persons
Insta

Blank Pages for Your Story

Blank Pages for Your Story

Blank Pages for Your Story

ABOUT THE AUTHORS

Marina L. Reed (honB.A., M.A., B.Ed.) grew up in rural Ontario. She has lived and worked around the world as an educator, journalist, writer, and artist. Author of 11 books, a freelance writer, ghostwriter, and producer/writer for CBC Television, Marina brings her skills as a writer to cocreate *Remember...It's OK*. She believes the empowerment of individuals is the first step toward healing ourselves and our communities. Follow her at *Marinalreed.com*.

Marian Grace Boyd (B.R.E., B.A.Psych, M.A. Counselling Psych.) was born in Switzerland, lived in Africa, and now lives just outside Toronto, Ontario. Marian has more than thirty years experience as a psychotherapist and grief counsellor and she is the founder of Griefwalk. She brings her formal training to cocreate *Remember...It's OK*. Marian is passionate about helping people find peace. Follow her on *Rememberitsok.com*.

Disclaimer

This book is designed to provide information and motivation to our readers. The authors are not obliged or committed to provide any type of psychological, legal, or other professional advice on a personal basis. The authors are not liable for any physical, psychological, emotional, or financial damages including but not limited to special, incidental, consequential, or other damages as a result of reading this book. The reader is responsible for his or her own choices, actions, and results.

TESTIMONIALS

I think that this book has really hit the nail on the head, so to speak. The teen years are an extremely difficult time for adolescents, and experiencing grief can be a time of confusion and perhaps even guilt for feeling emotions that aren't considered to be "normal." To make matters even more challenging, teens are often dismissed for the way they feel and are not given the proper help and resources they need to navigate their struggles. That certainly was my experience when I suffered loss. However, this book gives permission to the individual to feel the way they do and provides simple and practical outlets for dealing with their emotions such as music, physical practices, and mental exercises. In my own personal life, these moments recorded here remind me that healing is not a linear journey: there are ups and downs along the way, and it is perfectly normal and acceptable to experience such situations — there is no "typical" timeline at which you must deal with your grief. I wish I had had this book much earlier. I love that there are places to write my own thoughts and suggestions of what to put there.

These raw, personal accounts of tough situations give both parents and teachers the ability to view exactly the way some teens are feeling and just how vulnerable they feel; perhaps the causation of the common lack of dialogue between the two parties. This book will change that. I can't wait to share this book with a friend of mine who I know is struggling with a devastating loss. I feel that these stories will help him to see that healing is a process, and that it is OK to feel the hurt and pain that goes with it. It gives an alternate way of looking at grief and loss, to see that there are ways that it can be used for good, and to make yourself stronger from your experiences. Thank you for writing this book; it is something that doesn't get enough attention in today's culture and is a timely message for those who are hurting: that there is truly hope and a life to be lived after loss.

Kaitlyn Wierenga, a teen

I loved the style of this book. It really spoke to me. I loved how someone poured their heart out and received a reassuring response. You assured the reader that they will be OK, and it's completely normal to feel what they are feeling, no matter what the emotion. This will appeal to teens. Nobody wants to talk about their grief. Teen years are when we are trying to figure out who we are as a person, and when something in our life causes grief to happen, it makes things so much more confusing. This book will give teens the hope they need and want. As someone who has had their fair share of traumatic experiences, I found that this book is a tool I can use for comfort and to express myself with the blank page suggestions. I related to many of the moments shared and the advice that was given was extremely helpful. This would also help parents and teachers by giving them an insight on how the teen may be feeling and what it is they went through and what they want. Again, the blank page suggestions and Check It Out will be so helpful. I would definitely recommend this to a friend, not only for them to use if they need it but also as a way for them to understand what other teenagers are going through and that it is going to be OK!

Kayleigh Hart-Robertson, a teen

Red — Anger

Orange — ~~Satire~~ Satire

Yellow — & Happiness

green — Comfort

T — Confusion

Blue — Peace

Manufactured by Amazon.ca
Bolton, ON